Planning Successful Employee Performance

A Practical Guide To Planning
Individual Achievement

Karen R. Seeker
Joe B. Wilson

Jossey-Bass
Pfeiffer
San Francisco

RICHARD
CHANG
ASSOCIATES

Copyright © 1997 by Richard Chang Associates, Inc.

ISBN: 0-7879-5110-2

All rights reserved. No part of this publication, except those pages specifically marked "Reproducible Form," may be reproduced, stored in a retrieval system, or transmitted, in any form or by any means, electronic, mechanical, photocopying, recording, or otherwise, without the prior written permission of the publisher.

Printed in the United States of America

Published by

Jossey-Bass Pfeiffer
350 Sansome Street, 5th Floor
San Francisco, California 94104-1342
(415) 433-1740; Fax (415) 433-0499
(800) 274-4434; Fax (800) 569-0443

www.pfeiffer.com

Printing 10 9 8 7 6 5 4 3 2 1

ACKNOWLEDGMENTS

About The Authors

Karen R. Seeker, a Senior Consultant for Richard Chang Associates, Inc., is highly skilled in the areas of performance improvement, process management, reengineering, and strategic planning. For over 12 years she has led numerous commercial, government, and academic organizations to improve their performance, specializing in high-tech, research and development environments, as well as major corporate providers.

Joe B. Wilson, Managing Director of Consulting Services at Richard Chang Associates, Inc., is a Performance Management and Business Consultant with more than 20 years of international experience. His background in Organizational Management, and facilitation of training programs spans a wide range—from highly technical systems projects, to management/sales development, to Business Process Improvement implementations.

The authors would like to acknowledge the support of the entire team of professionals at Richard Chang Associates, Inc. for their contribution to the guidebook development process. In addition, special thanks are extended to the many client organizations who have helped us shape the practical ideas and proven methods shared in this guidebook.

Additional Credits

Editors:	Paul Jerome, Ruth Stingley, and Eva Shaw
Reviewers:	Rich Baisner, Shirley Codrey, Doug Dalziel Susan Parker, and Pamela Wade
Graphic Layout:	Dena Putnam and Christina Slater
Cover Design:	Eric Strand and John Odam Design Associates

PREFACE

The 1990's have already presented individuals and organizations with some very difficult challenges to face and overcome. So who will have the advantage as we move toward the year 2000 and beyond?

The advantage will belong to those with a commitment to continuous learning. Whether on an individual basis or as an entire organization, one key ingredient to building a continuous learning environment is *The Practical Guidebook Collection* brought to you by the Publications Division of Richard Chang Associates, Inc.

After understanding the future *"learning needs"* expressed by our clients and other potential customers, we are pleased to publish *The Practical Guidebook Collection*. These guidebooks are designed to provide you with proven, *"real-world"* tips, tools, and techniques—on a wide range of subjects—that you can apply in the workplace and/or on a personal level immediately.

Once you've had a chance to benefit from *The Practical Guidebook Collection*, please share your feedback with us. We've included a brief *Evaluation and Feedback Form* at the end of the guidebook that you can fax to us at (714) 727-7007.

With your feedback, we can continuously improve the resources we are providing through the Publications Division of Richard Chang Associates, Inc.

Wishing you successful reading,

Richard Y. Chang
President and CEO
Richard Chang Associates, Inc.

Table Of Contents

1. Introduction 1
   Why Read This Guidebook?
   What's In It For You?
   Who Should Read This Guidebook?
   When And How To Use It

2. The Big Picture 5
   The Performance Management Cycle
   The Performance Planning Model
   Position Descriptions
   Performance Objectives
   Performance Action Plans

3. Incorporating Inputs Into The Individual Performance Plan 23
   Gathering And Understanding Organizational And Work Group Performance Inputs
   Considering New Requirements And Needs
   Utilizing Previous Performance Evaluations And Position Descriptions

4. Communicating Performance-Planning Inputs To Team Members 35
   The Importance Of Communicating
   How Will You Communicate This Information?
   What Will You Communicate?
   Overcoming Resistance
   After The Meeting

5. The Position Description 45
   The One-On-One Meeting
   The Importance Of The Position Description
   Drafting And Revising Your Position Description

6. **Performance Objectives And Performance Action Plans** 65
   Defining Performance Objectives
   Types Of Performance Objectives
   Drafting Your Performance Action Plans

7. **Finalizing The Performance Plan** 83
   Where You Should Be
   Finalizing The Plan
   Preparing To Negotiate
   The Performance Plan As An Agreement

8. **Summary** 95

   Appendix:
   Reference Material 97

*"Lots of folks confuse
bad management with destiny."*

K. Hubbard

CHAPTER ONE

INTRODUCTION

Why Read This Guidebook?

Planning is necessary. There's no way around it. You've seen and experienced the results of both adequate and inadequate planning. Whether you're planning something as simple as a child's birthday party, or as complex as an investment portfolio, planning is absolutely indispensable. It keeps you on track and steers you toward success.

The lessons you have learned in life regarding effective planning also apply to work situations. Once you've completed a troublesome project at work, have you ever wished that you had a better plan for getting the job done more efficiently, more effectively, or without the added stress?

Or what about plans regarding your employees? Have you ever considered how much more you could accomplish if you actually helped them plan for their success? More than likely you have, or you wouldn't have opened this guidebook.

Planning Successful Employee Performance provides you with an effective system to implement performance planning. It will help you set employee expectations and provide the means by which you can evaluate employee performance. This guidebook also will introduce you to the Performance Planning Model, and it will guide you through its four easy-to-apply steps.

Applying the Performance Planning Model enables you to plan for improved individual performance. The employee performance plans you create will result in individual and organizational success, because they are linked directly to high-priority performance targets.

INTRODUCTION

What's In It For You?

As with any planning strategy, this process may appear cumbersome and unnecessary. The truth is that completing the planning steps doesn't take that long, and the benefits you gain are numerous.

When you don't plan, you may save time up front, but you also may face pitfalls and unnecessary detours. Wouldn't you rather be known as a wise investor of your organization's time?

More specifically, be assured that as performance planning is integrated into your work process with your employees, you can expect to see improvements faster than you may imagine. When expectations are conveyed clearly, and a sense of unity and purpose is created, miracles can happen. For example, by clarifying job expectations, your staff will be more focused. Productivity will lead to satisfaction and higher motivation. Profits improve. And your organization prospers.

In addition, there will be no more comparing apples to oranges when evaluation time arrives; everyone in your organization will be using the same planning, measurement, and evaluation methods. You'll all be playing the same sport with the same rule book. The Performance Planning Model provides a sound structure upon which an organization—your work group—can thrive.

INTRODUCTION

Who Should Read This Guidebook?

Planning Successful Employee Performance will benefit anyone who is concerned with, or responsible for, the performance of individuals. It is written for team leaders, executives, managers, supervisors, administrators, human resource personnel, and trainers. Personnel with nonprofit organizations and government agencies will also benefit from modeling the techniques found in this guidebook.

Regardless of whether you are in a service-related field, high-technology, or a manufacturing environment, this guidebook is for individuals who have influence over the destiny of themselves, their work, and their employees.

When And How To Use It

Ideally, the concepts in this guidebook should be used early on in your organization's planning process. In a perfect world, you would plan for performance success before you recruited or hired any employees.

In reality, you are more likely to be saddled with inherited budget constraints, production hurdles, and personnel riddles. Planning is often not even in the picture. Sometimes, it may even seem that you have to be a magician and pull rabbits out of a hat.

So, since living in a perfect world isn't an option, you can use the planning model presented in this guidebook to tie into the priorities and goals of your organization. The Performance Planning Model is proactive. It will help you anticipate obstacles, and it works.

Remember: when you plan for employee success, you are better able to measure and meet performance expectations. And when the actions of your employees are closely in sync with the organization's, you're more likely to have a successful trip. So buckle up and plan for success. You're on the right road.

CHAPTER TWO

THE BIG PICTURE

While planning for your employees' successful performance is absolutely necessary, it can't guarantee high performance. Think of it in the following way.

No matter how extensively or carefully you plan for a party, if you don't follow through and see to it that you're accomplishing what you planned for, it won't be a success. For managers, supervisors, and anyone in charge of other individuals, planning is the first phase of a three-phase cycle—the Performance Management Cycle. And while planning alone can't carry you to the high-performance finish line, it can get you off to a great start.

The Performance Management Cycle

The Performance Management Cycle consists of three phases—Planning, Coaching, and Evaluating.

THE BIG PICTURE

Planning involves defining and discussing roles, responsibilities, and measurable expectations. That leads to Coaching—where employees are mentored and developed—reinforcing or redirecting their efforts through support, feedback, and recognition. Then, in the Evaluating Phase, the employees' actual performance is reviewed and compared to expectations established in their performance plans. Plans are enhanced, the cycle repeats, and the employee, manager, team, and organization continue to learn and grow.

PERFORMANCE MANAGEMENT CYCLE

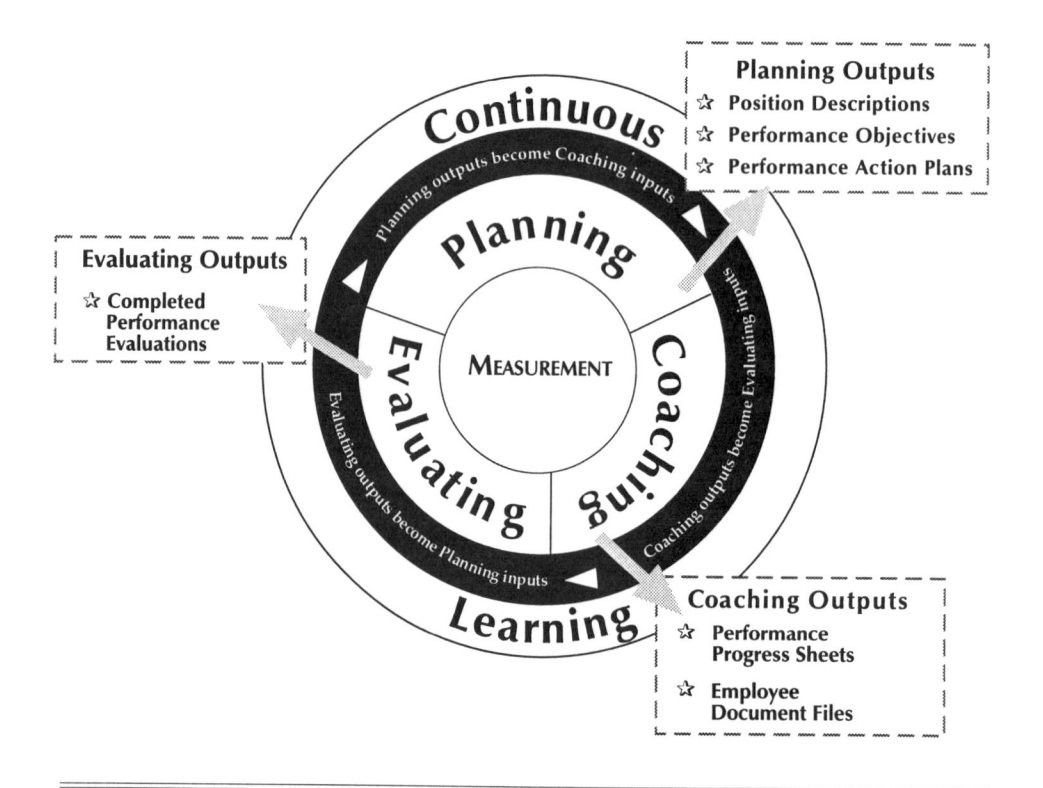

Continuous **Planning** *Coaching* **Evaluating** *Learning*

MEASUREMENT

Planning outputs become Coaching inputs
Coaching outputs become Evaluating inputs
Evaluating outputs become Planning inputs

Planning Outputs
- ☆ Position Descriptions
- ☆ Performance Objectives
- ☆ Performance Action Plans

Coaching Outputs
- ☆ Performance Progress Sheets
- ☆ Employee Document Files

Evaluating Outputs
- ☆ Completed Performance Evaluations

PLANNING SUCCESSFUL EMPLOYEE PERFORMANCE

THE BIG PICTURE

Each phase is based on input from the previous phase and produces an output, which in turn, serves as an input for the next phase.

All three phases of the Performance Management Cycle are equally critical to the quality of this process. Please bear in mind that each phase feeds upon the other; therefore, they should be treated sequentially. Planning comes first, then Coaching, and finally Evaluating. Other practical guidebooks published by Richard Chang Associates, Inc. that provide additional insight into the Performance Management Cycle include *Coaching For Peak Employee Performance, Coaching Through Effective Feedback, Evaluating Employee Performance,* and *Interviewing And Selecting High Performers.*

The Performance Management Cycle is the implementation of the final steps in the Measurement Linkage Model. This model is discussed in *Measuring Organizational Improvement Impact,* a guidebook *(also published by Richard Chang Associates, Inc.)* that deals with determining corporate and work group level Key Result Areas *(KRAs)* and Key Indicators *(KIs)* of success. Key Result Areas *(KRAs)* are critical, *"must achieve," "make or break,"* performance categories for an organization. Key Indicators *(KIs)* are specific measures which help determine how well you are performing in a given KRA. Note that the Planning Phase takes place between Steps 7 and 8 of the Measurement Linkage Model *(see model on the next page).*

Step 7 of the model—*"Establish work group 'objectives' and 'tactics'"*— serves as one input into the Performance Planning Model. Then, in the Planning Phase, employee plans are drafted and revised, and they are implemented fully in the Coaching Phase *(which begins Step 8 of the Measurement Linkage Model).*

THE BIG PICTURE

MEASUREMENT LINKAGE MODEL

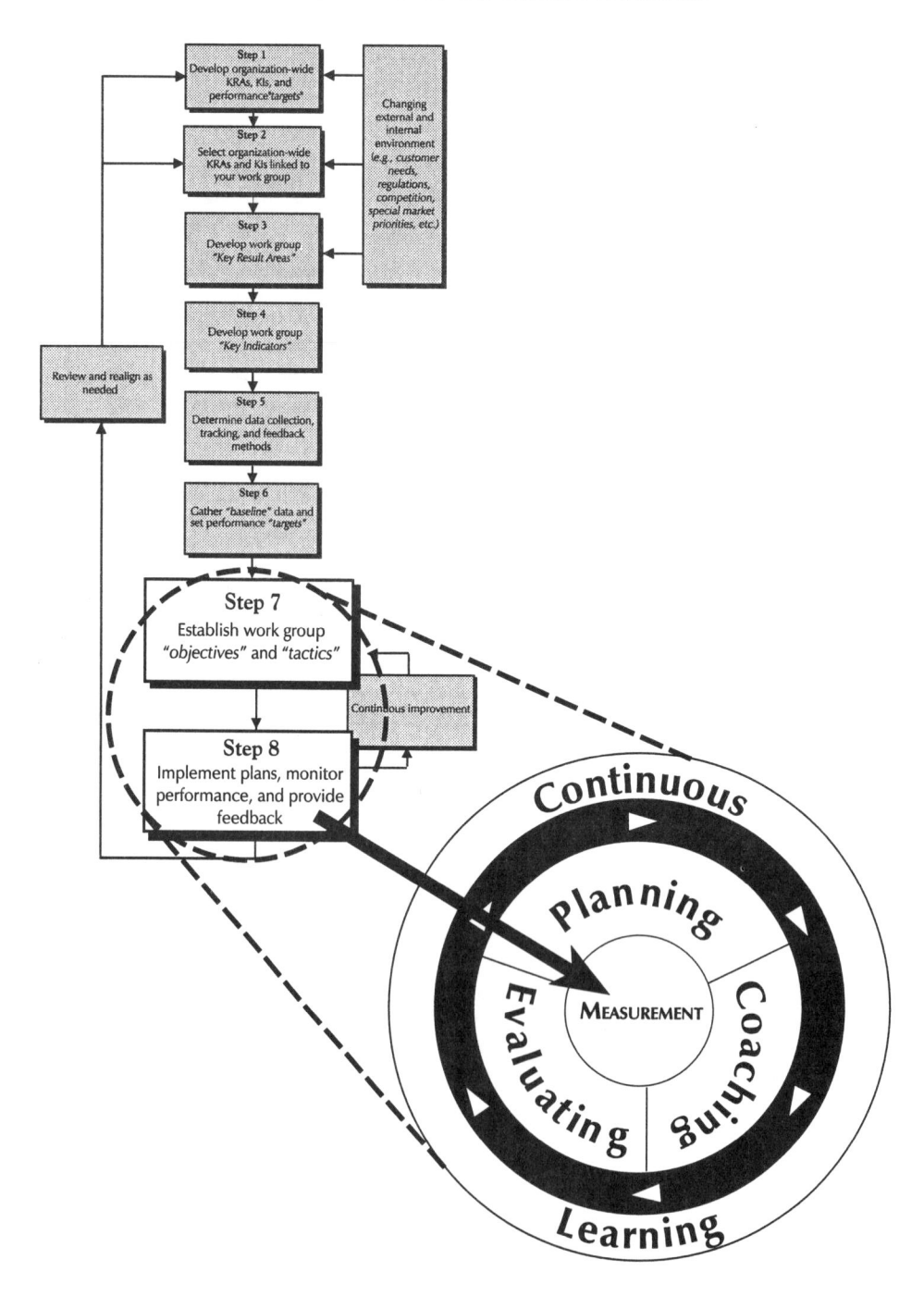

Step 1 — Develop organization-wide KRAs, KIs, and performance "targets"

Step 2 — Select organization-wide KRAs and KIs linked to your work group

Step 3 — Develop work group "Key Result Areas"

Step 4 — Develop work group "Key Indicators"

Step 5 — Determine data collection, tracking, and feedback methods

Step 6 — Gather "baseline" data and set performance "targets"

Step 7 — Establish work group "objectives" and "tactics"

Step 8 — Implement plans, monitor performance, and provide feedback

Changing external and internal environment (e.g., customer needs, regulations, competition, special market priorities, etc.)

Review and realign as needed

Continuous improvement

Continuous — Planning, Coaching, Learning, Evaluating — **MEASUREMENT**

THE BIG PICTURE

Why even discuss the Measurement Linkage Model? Because you cannot plan for individual performance adequately unless you have already established work group objectives and tactics.

Work group objectives and tactics:

- Provide direction for employee work
- Allow you to identify and develop individual employee skills that are valuable to your organization
- Provide you with a means for measuring employee performance

Measuring Organizational Improvement Impact focuses on planning and evaluating organization-wide performance. *Planning Successful Employee Performance* focuses on improving individual performance that contributes directly to organizational performance. The two are closely aligned.

Note: Throughout this guidebook, *"work group"* and *"team"* will be used interchangeably to mean the staff members of your department, division, a special-purpose committee, a task force, etc. The people on your staff are defined as team members, which is also the same as employees, associates, and group members. Likewise, managers and supervisors sometimes are referred to as team leaders.

Jake's Market, Inc., a chain of specialty grocery stores...

is growing quickly. There are twenty-three stores in the organization that are located throughout the western states, and fifteen are slated to open in the next fiscal year. Headquarters has plans to dominate the specialty food market in the south and mid-Atlantic states within the next few years.

Jake's is a progressive corporation. High-level management encourages entrepreneurial spirit at individual stores. Every year, store managers work with headquarters to establish and reinforce organization-wide KRAs and KIs. In turn, these managers create work group KRAs and KIs to define and measure how they contribute toward success in their particular store.

THE BIG PICTURE

Terry Ling is the manager at a west coast store that has twenty employees, some full time and others who work on a part-time basis. Her management team consists of herself; Milt Chandler, her assistant; and P.J. Richfield, the night manager. Terry is proud of her position and her team of employees; however, there are times when she knows that her team could be more effective.

Recently, headquarters implemented a new planning strategy, and Terry is excited about the prospect. One of the corporate-level KRAs established for this fiscal year is *"Customer Loyalty."* As Terry recently told a new stock clerk, *"We are dedicated to provide all our customers with old-fashioned service and state-of-the-art quality, every day. We are clearly not just another upscale supermarket."*

Because of the organization's commitment to customers, Terry called her managers together to discuss an appropriate KRA for their work group that would support the organizational one. *"Customer loyalty is the top concern among those at headquarters,"* she said. *"And one KI that measures customer loyalty is 'percent of customer-retention rate.'"*

"And just what is the customer-retention rate?" asked P.J.

Terry smiled. She knew P.J. was always interested in improvement. *"At the corporate level,"* Terry answered, *"they baselined the current customer-retention rate at 80 percent, as defined by customers who visit the stores six or more times per quarter. Headquarters set a performance target of 85 percent by year end."*

"Then we need to get to work on our customer-retention rate right away," P.J. said.

Together, Terry and her staff decided to adopt the same KRA and KI for their store. Terry's store currently had a 75 percent retention rate, which they knew from their quarterly customer interviews. Therefore, they set a performance target of achieving a 90 percent customer-retention rate by year end.

"At headquarters," Terry explained, *"we learned how to write specific performance plans for each employee that will help us achieve our targets. I thought it was a great idea,"* she said. *"So, once we have a store-wide meeting about our store-level KRAs and our thinking thus far, we need to meet with the employees individually to draft their plans. Then, and only then, can we work together to perform in the way we wish."*

"Sounds pretty complicated," P.J. replied. *"But I'll back you up. Especially if it means that our employees will work better."*...

Throughout the next chapters, Terry and her staff will develop individual performance plans using the Performance Planning Model.

The Performance Planning Model

As mentioned earlier, performance planning ties together individual, team, and organizational performance targets. The linking of these targets is the first step of the Performance Planning Model.

The Performance Planning Model has four major steps:

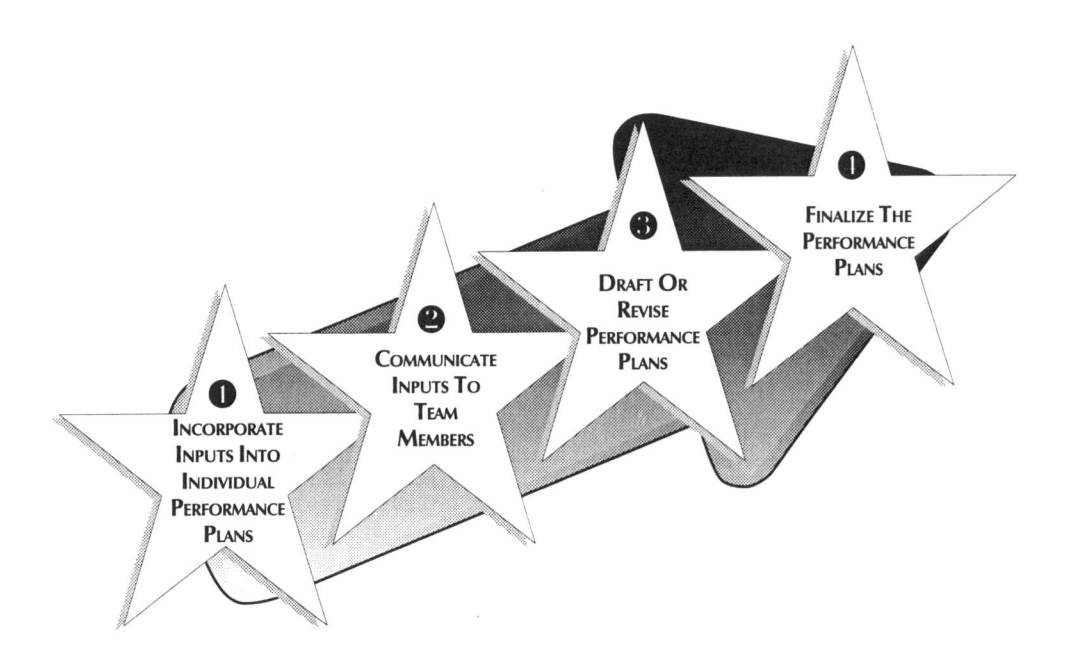

1. Incorporate Inputs Into Individual Performance Plans
2. Communicate Inputs To Team Members
3. Draft Or Revise Performance Plans
4. Finalize The Performance Plans

The Performance Planning Model provides a step-by-step process for producing individual performance plans.

In the first step, you will incorporate the information necessary to produce effective plans. In the second step, you'll convey the general information you would like to include in the performance plans on both team and individual levels, and reflect on the new plans. In the third step, you will actually draft the individual plans. In the fourth step, you'll have an opportunity to negotiate and finalize the plans.

THE BIG PICTURE

When you follow the Performance Planning Model, you will develop a tailored performance plan for each of your team members. This plan will take into consideration each team member's particular skills, knowledge, and abilities. It will also detail each individual's specific responsibilities required in order to achieve your work group's objectives and tactics. Invest whatever time you have, and you will reap the benefits of successful performance that leads to organizational achievement.

Before you begin with the first step of the Performance Planning Model, it's helpful to take a look at the components of a performance plan. In short, a performance plan provides individual team members job expectations for the upcoming year.

The plans you will be creating consist of three major components:

- Position Descriptions
- Performance Objectives
- Performance Action Plans

Suggested formats for each component that you can reproduce and use in your planning efforts can be found in the appendix of this guidebook.

Position Descriptions

For each job family, classification, or general position within your work group, you will develop *(or request from your Human Resources department, if it already exists)* a Position Description. The Position Description defines the general playing field per job family *(e.g., you may need only one Position Description for all entry-level customer service representatives)*. In other words, it is a generic listing of key responsibilities, required skills, performance measurements, evaluation methods, and required education and experience.

If you develop accurate Position Descriptions, both you and your employees will benefit. Why? Because all parties involved will have a common understanding of, and expectations for, the responsibilities of the position. They'll also know the ideal mix of skills, education, and experience needed for the position. And, since a description of how each key responsibility will be evaluated is included, there'll be no surprises and *(hopefully!)* no complaints when evaluation time rolls around.

This type of description is more comprehensive than most traditional Job Descriptions, which typically do not include skills, education, and experience needed, nor do they define the key measurements that will determine success on the job. Without these, there is no clear, agreed-upon, determination of success that both you and your employees can use to guide their day-to-day performance. Furthermore, with this added information, the Position Description becomes a useful tool for you to use during interviewing, selecting, and training new employees.

THE BIG PICTURE

POSITION DESCRIPTION

JOB FAMILY/POSITION:	SALARY BAND:	DEPARTMENT:	ORIGINATED:	REVISED:

RESPONSIBILITIES	SKILL CODES	MEASUREMENT CODES	EVALUATION METHOD CODES
1.			
2.			
3.			
4.			
5.			
6.			
7.			
8.			
9.			
10.			

THE BIG PICTURE

Code	SKILLS (Observable Behaviors, Not Traits/Values)
S1	
S2	
S3	
S4	
S5	
S6	
S7	
S8	

Code	Measurements	Code	Evaluation Methods	Education/Experience
M1		E1		1.
M2		E2		2.
M3		E3		3.
M4		E4		4.
M5		E5		5.
M6		E6		6.
M7		E7		7.
M8		E8		8.

THE BIG PICTURE

Performance Objectives

The second component of a performance plan is a list of Performance Objectives you and each individual employee will create together. Performance Objectives take the Position Description a step further. They help link individual performance to team objectives and tactics. Whereas the Position Description defines the on-going key responsibilities of the position, Performance Objectives have a beginning and an end. Performance Objectives are statements of conditions that will exist after work is performed, and that can be measured quantitatively.

Performance Objectives must be aligned, relevant, and value-added. *(You'll be given information about how to write effective Performance Objectives in another chapter.)* They also must be tied to team tactics and goals, which is part of the first step of the Performance Planning Model.

Performance Action Plans

For selected Performance Objectives, team members may find it necessary and beneficial to draft a specific plan of action. These Performance Action Plans help team members delineate key actions and milestones, deliverables and results, any resources required, the risks involved, and any contingency plans related to achieving the objectives.

The Performance Action Plan clarifies all expectations and concerns up front. Team members should have a clear idea of what is required of them. The benefit? Valuable resources are effectively tapped, not wasted. Because you know the capabilities and potential of each individual team member and you know what objectives and tactics support your organization, you can strategically plan for success.

THE BIG PICTURE

PERFORMANCE OBJECTIVES

EMPLOYEE:	POSITION:	DEPARTMENT:	SUPERVISOR:

TYPES OF PERFORMANCE OBJECTIVES: PROJECT PROCESS BUSINESS-AS-USUAL CORE VALUES

ORIGINATED: **REVISED:**

OBJECTIVE	TYPE	TARGET DATE

EMPLOYEE SIGNATURE: DATE:

SUPERVISOR SIGNATURE: DATE:

THE BIG PICTURE

PERFORMANCE ACTION PLAN				
Employee:	**Position:**	**Department:**	**Supervisor:**	
Performance Objective:			**Originated:**	**Revised:**

Actions/Milestones	Deliverables/Results	Required Resources
1.		
2.		
3.		
4.		

Risks, Impacts And Likelihood (High, Medium, Low)	Options And Recommendations
Risk: **Impacts:** **Likelihood:**	
Risk: **Impacts:** **Likelihood:**	
Risk: **Impacts:** **Likelihood:**	

THE BIG PICTURE

> *Late the next afternoon...*
> Terry, Milt, and P.J. were discussing performance planning for the positions of "Cashier" and "Stocker." P.J. scratched her head. *"Does the Performance Planning Model help us come up with a performance plan for each individual employee, or is it a plan for the store?"*
>
> *"We build a plan for each team member in our store,"* said Milt. He began scrutinizing the worksheets spread out on Terry's desk. *"It's all right here. The performance plan has three parts: a Position Description, the Performance Objectives, and the Performance Action Plans. But, it does sound like a lot of work to me."*
>
> Terry nodded. *"It can be, but it's important. Think about it. The performance plan helps us address team members' skills and abilities and specific responsibilities so that each member can contribute to the work group's objectives and tactics,"* she explained.
>
> As P.J. and Milt looked at the worksheets, Terry continued her explanation, *"Let's look at the description for the job family of 'cashier,' since it desperately needs to be rewritten—it's completely out of date. We need to do it anyway, since our new cashier, Bevy Klein, needs Performance Objectives and a Performance Action Plan. We can't expect to measure and evaluate performance without providing the tools to help her succeed. We want her to have a good start at Jake's."*
>
> P.J. glanced at her watch. *"Well, it's off to the cash registers for me. I'm covering for a cashier who is taking a final exam tonight. But one more question, Terry. Will you be going through the Performance Planning Model with everyone?"*
>
> *"Absolutely,"* Terry answered, as they all got up to leave. *"I'll be holding shift meetings next week."*

Once these plans are implemented, employee performance will be measured throughout the performance period. The performance plans you create will be valuable and workable, and they will provide you with a means to measure performance.

Now that you know what you will be working toward, it's time to delve into the Performance Planning Model and see exactly what that work entails. Don't delay. Your efforts will result in improved performance from your team members sooner than you may think!

Chapter Two Worksheet: Looking At The Big Picture

1. How does the performance management process at your company differ from the Performance Management Cycle presented in this chapter?

   _____
   _____
   _____
   _____
   _____
   _____

2. Which elements of the performance management cycle would, if implemented, most likely have the biggest impact on your organization's success?

   _____
   _____
   _____
   _____
   _____
   _____

THE BIG PICTURE

3. Briefly describe your organization's current approach for individual performance planning *(including specific processes and forms)*.

CHAPTER THREE

INCORPORATING INPUTS INTO THE INDIVIDUAL PERFORMANCE PLAN

The performance plans you create for your team members don't materialize out of nowhere. You could, supposedly, sit down and write Position Descriptions, Performance Objectives, and Performance Action Plans for your employees without researching and incorporating all the necessary inputs. However, it's doubtful such performance plans would achieve results that make a difference.

The first step in the Performance Planning Model involves incorporating the correct inputs into the individualized performance plan. This step is basically a research-and-preparation step, in which you collect vital information and use it to your advantage.

This information comes from four major input areas:

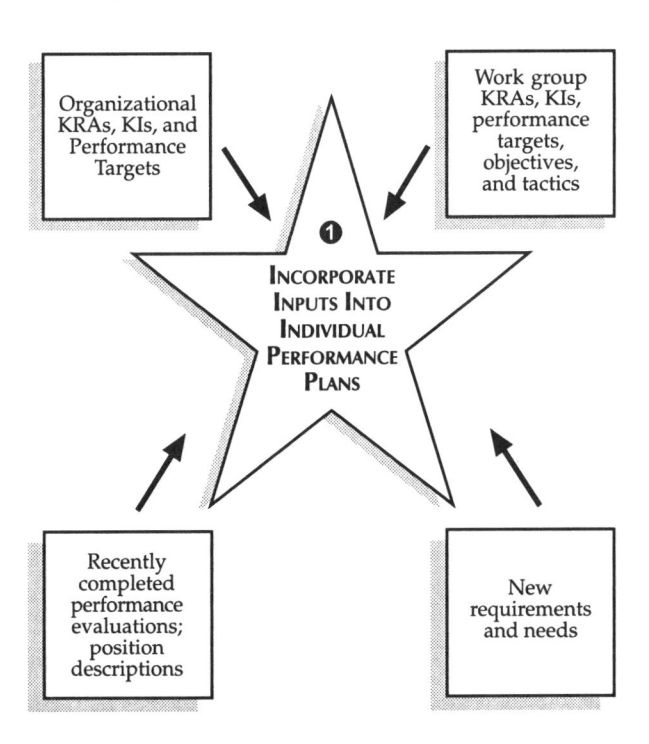

```
        Organizational                    Work group
        KRAs, KIs, and                    KRAs, KIs,
        Performance                       performance
        Targets                           targets,
                                          objectives,
                                          and tactics

                    ❶ INCORPORATE
                      INPUTS INTO
                      INDIVIDUAL
                      PERFORMANCE
                      PLANS

        Recently
        completed                         New
        performance                       requirements
        evaluations;                      and needs
        position
        descriptions
```

INCORPORATING INPUTS

Gathering And Understanding Organizational And Work Group Performance Inputs

At the management level, you should now have an understanding of what your organizational Key Result Areas and Key Indicators are and how to achieve them. If you don't *(e.g., because no one has ever identified them)*, then you must conduct planning based on what you believe is important to your organization.

Once you and your team understand where your organization is headed, you should proceed to come up with your own work group KRAs and KIs, gather baseline measures, set your own performance targets, develop work group objectives, and identify tactics to achieve those objectives.

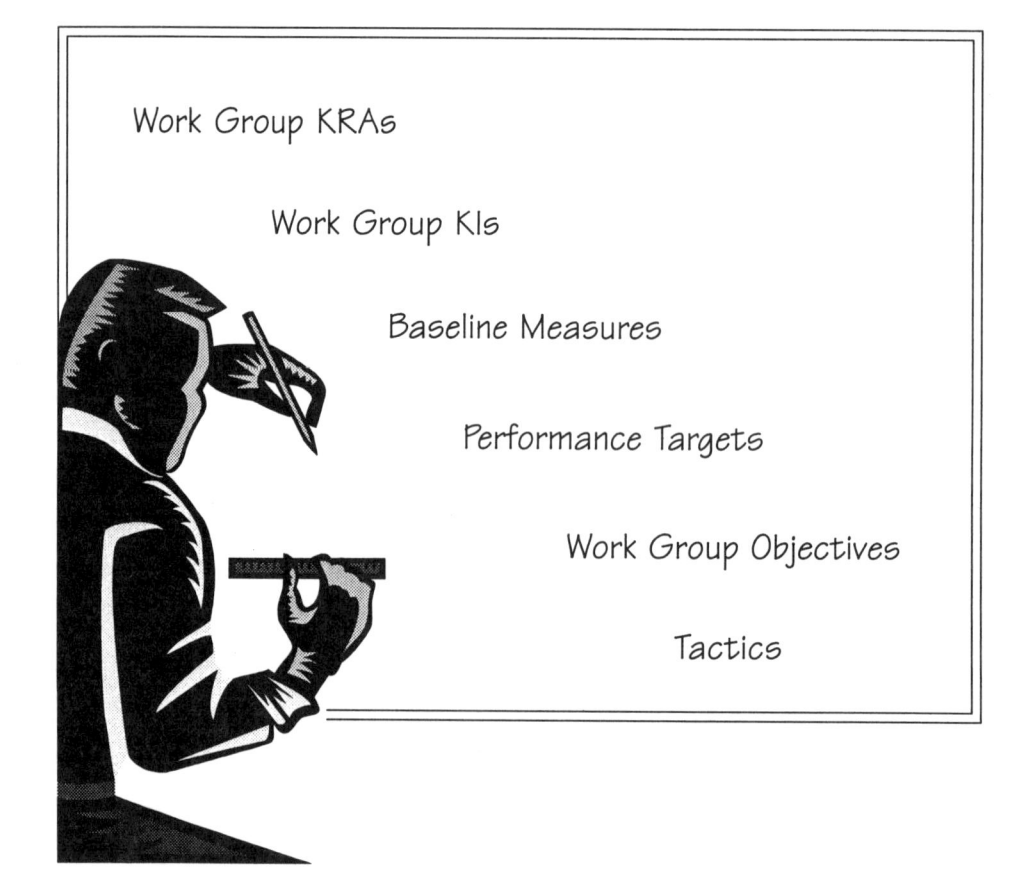

Work Group KRAs

Work Group KIs

Baseline Measures

Performance Targets

Work Group Objectives

Tactics

INCORPORATING INPUTS

```
                    Organization-Wide
                    Strategic Planning
```

Organizational Level

- KRA → KI → KI → KI
- KRA → KI → KI
- KRA → KI → KI → KI

Work Group Level

KRA → KI, KI → Performance Target, Performance Target → Objective (Tactic, Tactic) → Objective (Tactic, Tactic) → Objective (Tactic, Tactic)

Work Group Level

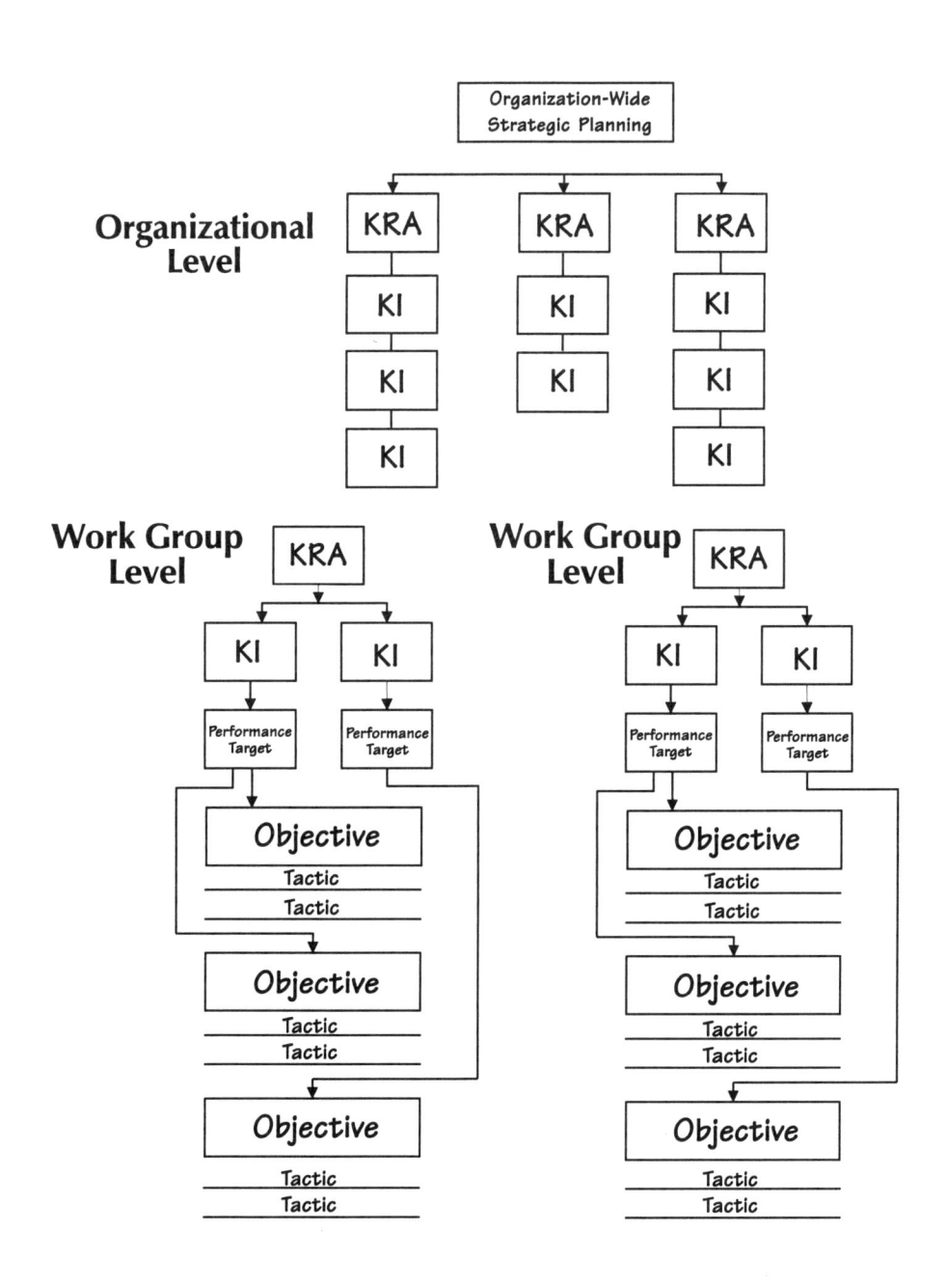

KRA → KI, KI → Performance Target, Performance Target → Objective (Tactic, Tactic) → Objective (Tactic, Tactic) → Objective (Tactic, Tactic)

If you follow this process, you'll come up with Performance Objectives and Performance Action Plans for each employee that reflect the direction in which your organization is headed.

INCORPORATING INPUTS

The next afternoon,...

P.J. and Milt clustered around Terry's desk. *"I'm pleased that we've set a performance target of a 90 percent customer-retention rate by the year's end,"* Terry said. *"Doing so will support headquarter's KRA of increasing customer loyalty."*

"But retaining customers isn't as simple as it appears," Milt interjected. *"Greeting them and chatting with them is great, but if we take too long at the checkout stands, they get crabby. All the smiling in the world won't help at that point."*

"You're right, Milt," Terry responded. *"Decreasing checkout time will have a direct impact on increasing customer loyalty and improving our customer-retention rate."* Terry stopped for a moment, grabbed a piece of paper, and started scribbling.

"One thing I learned at headquarters was that coming up with objectives to achieve a KRA can be complex. If the objective we choose is straightforward, then it helps identify our tactics and plans. It sounds like you may have hit on an important one—decreasing checkout time. Let's formalize that idea by saying that one primary work group objective for next year is to decrease the checkout time by 20 percent by the end of the third quarter."

P.J. interrupted with, *"But decreasing checkout time can't be done without figuring out how long our checkout time is and why it's too long."*

"Exactly," Terry replied. *"We have to figure out what we need to work on to decrease checkout time. The actions we choose, then, become our tactics which will feed our individual performance plans."*

"So each position in the store needs to think about how their job needs to change over the next year to support our objective of decreasing checkout time?" Milt asked. *"After all, most of us contribute in some way to the time it takes for customers to find the products they need, purchase the products, get them into bags, and leave the store."*

"You hit the nail right on the head," Terry replied. *"The process of decreasing checkout time involves all of us in some way. We must make sure that we all have the skills needed and are supported in other ways. The skills must be added to the new Position Descriptions and be reflected in the Performance Objectives and Performance Action Plans."*

As the management team continued its discussion, Terry smiled to herself. The KRAs, KIs, performance targets, objectives, and tactics all would provide important information for the creation of each team member's performance plan. Even Milt seemed a little more accepting of the process....

Considering New Requirements And Needs

Some aspects that affect your business may not be included or reflected in your organization's current KRAs and KIs. Nevertheless, they are important to organization-wide management and, therefore, need to be accounted for in your performance plans. Usually, new requirements and needs involve outside influences—new marketplace trends, technological advances, or competitive pressure.

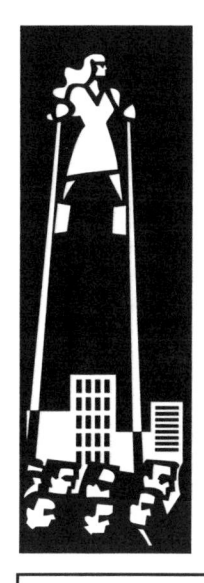

As with any organizational plan, it is necessary to periodically *"take stock"* of the overall market environment. Ideally, this should occur at the beginning of the planning cycle, no matter how often this cycle occurs *(usually annually)*. This is the time when new requirements need to be integrated into the organization's plan. These requirements could range anywhere from keeping up with the competition to implementing new programs or procedures.

To consider new requirements and needs, ask yourself and your team members:

- ◆ What's our competition doing that's different from us?
- ◆ Is it better than what we're doing?
- ◆ What's happening in the world or our immediate environment that may impact the way we do things?

INCORPORATING INPUTS

For the most part, performance planning is a proactive process based on current organizational priorities. However, you must look at the market carefully to understand new requirements that can be included in the Position Description, Performance Objectives, and/or Performance Action Plans you create for each individual employee.

For example, one organization's shipping department determined that not only was there a new market need for the ability to track products throughout the shipping process, but also, that market trends indicated a higher demand for overnight shipping. Based on these new requirements, the manager of the shipping department created new objectives and tactics.

Objective # 1: To develop the capability to enable customers to self-track merchandise by end of year.

Tactics:

- Research and purchase a software package
- Design customer training for using the software

Objective # 2: To create a strategic alliance with an overnight carrier by end of the second quarter.

Tactics:

- Develop and distribute a request for a proposal
- Evaluate proposals and negotiate an agreement

INCORPORATING INPUTS

These objectives and tactics were written into the team members' Performance Objectives and Performance Action Plans. If you, too, are aware of new requirements and needs, you can include them in your employees' performance plans and watch your organization benefit.

> ### Bevy Klein, a new cashier at Jake's,...
> overheard the management team discussing the checkout time as she was returning from break. *"Excuse me for listening,"* she said, *"but at Super Store—where I worked before coming to Jake's—we had product scanners. Corporate never trained us, and it was a nightmare at first. Guess they thought we'd magically know how to use the equipment. But eventually, it did streamline the checkout process."*
>
> *"I also understand that Super Store is moving to electronic debit-card machines,"* P.J. commented. *"That way customers can use their bank cards instead of writing checks. Maybe we should consider them."*
>
> *"Good suggestions,"* said Terry. *"In order to keep up with technology and other stores, we need to investigate the possibility of becoming more high-tech. So, new scanning equipment and debit-card machines, along with training will be required. We really have a lot of work ahead of us!"...*

Utilizing Previous Performance Evaluations And Position Descriptions

Another aspect that needs to be included in the researching of your performance plan inputs is information from the last year's performance evaluations of your team members.

The completed performance evaluation is the ideal transition point for change and growth. Hopefully, each team member's performance has been acceptable within the scope of previously-targeted Performance Objectives. If so, now is the time for congratulations and further goal-setting.

INCORPORATING INPUTS

If this is your first effort at planning for successful employee performance, then the performance evaluation can indicate areas you need to develop as Performance Objectives. Sometimes a glowing performance evaluation means you can add additional challenges and tactics to the team member's performance plan.

Obviously, new employees or those filling new positions will not have a completed performance evaluation. If this is the case, simply continue on with the steps in the Performance Planning Model. By the end of the Performance Management Cycle, when you have completed the Evaluating Phase, you will have a completed performance evaluation to use in planning for the following year. Also, if you are beginning to plan for successful employee performance for the first time, you will need to:

- Look at the current Position Description for each position represented in your department or work group.

- Then, see if it still correlates with what each team member currently does on the job, and with what you envision the members of your work group doing.

If this is a new position for which you are planning, you won't have the luxury of reworking a current Position Description. So, you'll have to start from scratch.

Many times, Position Descriptions are completed in association with Human Resource personnel. It is important to work together in defining the Position Description so they will directly reflect your personnel requirements.

INCORPORATING INPUTS

Later that week,...

Terry and P.J. took out the file of performance evaluations from the previous year. Since Terry was the day manager and P.J. was the night manager, they divided the evaluations between the day and night shifts and each took the appropriate stack. Terry sent Milt over to her file cabinet to find Position Descriptions for all of the positions at Jake's.

"What are the performance evaluations supposed to tell us?" P.J. asked. *"I have one for most of the night employees, but not for Bevy, the new cashier, nor for two of our new stockers."*

"The performance evaluations should tell us how well the employee performed last year relative to the agreed-upon plans. This will help us determine plans for the upcoming year," Terry answered.

"But we have work to do to get to that point," P.J. commented, as Milt threw down a pile of papers on Terry's desk.

"Are these our Position Descriptions?" Terry asked. She picked one up and frowned.

"Pretty sad looking, aren't they?" Milt commented. *"Did headquarters actually spend money writing these up or did they copy them from some other store?"*

Terry, P.J., and Milt went through each of the Position Descriptions together and crossed out what no longer applied. They made notes about new responsibilities. *"I have new forms from headquarters we can use for this process,"* Terry said. *"And we'll meet with each job family of employees to create brand new Position Descriptions. They'll be much better. Just wait and see."*

The first step of the Performance Planning Model can be complex. Don't try to complete it in haste. Establish your work group objectives and tactics, consider new requirements and needs, and plug the information you glean from previous performance reviews and Position Descriptions into your performance plans. It's a *"must-do"* if you want to plan for successful employee performance.

Chapter Three Worksheet: Researching For Optimum Planning

1. Look at the following examples of Key Result Areas *(KRAs)* and Key Indicators *(KIs)*:

    KRA 1: Quality
    KI 1: Defects/units of production
    KI 2: Order fulfillment cycle time
    KI 3: Number of correct shipments/total shipments

    KRA 2: Innovation
    KI 1: Number of new product concepts in review
    KI 2: Number of suggestions submitted by employees/total number of employees
    KI 3: Number of suggestions implemented/total number of employees
    KI 4: Number of new products to market in the last 12 months/total products available

    Next, list one of your departmental or team KRAs, and a KI that measures it.

    KRA: _____

    KI: _____

2. Finally, list two work group objectives and tactics *(linked to the KI above)* that would help achieve each objective.

    Objective #1:

    _____

    Tactics:

    _____

    _____

INCORPORATING INPUTS

Objective #2:

_____

Tactics:

_____
_____

3. What new market requirements and needs *(including competitive influences)* are impacting the work your department or work group does?

_____
_____
_____
_____
_____
_____
_____

CHAPTER FOUR

COMMUNICATING PERFORMANCE-PLANNING INPUTS TO TEAM MEMBERS

Communication is essential in both personal and professional situations. How confident would you feel flying in an airplane in which the pilot and crew were not communicating effectively? Certainly, the absence of communication in an organization is not a life-or-death situation, but it can mean the difference between success or failure, especially in performance planning.

The Importance Of Communicating

In the second step of performance planning, you must design and conduct a team meeting to present your intentions and those of the organization. Keep in mind that clear, precise, supportive communication at organizational and work group levels will set the stage for developing meaningful individual performance plans later.

❷ COMMUNICATE INPUTS TO TEAM MEMBERS

This team meeting should illustrate what is expected at both the team and individual levels. In other words, you will be explaining the various performance planning inputs and discussing Position Descriptions for the different job families, as well as setting the stage for creating individual performance plans.

COMMUNICATING PLANNING INPUTS

How Will You Communicate This Information?

It is common knowledge that *"how"* you say something is often as important as *"what"* you say. That is why, in planning your team meeting, you need to consider every aspect of your presentation very carefully.

Before you do anything else, you must understand the characteristics of your audience. Will you be speaking to a group of computer programmers, salespeople, or Research and Development staff? Points that will appeal to members of one group may be meaningless to others. In addition, you must assess the different levels within that group, accounting for diversity, time on the job *(seniority)*, work styles, personalities, and so forth.

It is best to aim for making your presentation accessible for all levels within the team—strike a *"happy medium"* when creating overheads, handouts, and other presentation aids. What you include in your presentation is up to you. However, it has been shown that most adults retain and learn better from visual material than from any other type. For this reason, consider using previously-prepared flip charts, as well as overheads, slides, a video tape, or a multimedia presentation.

No matter what, you will need to prepare handouts, even if they contain nothing more than a graphic example of objectives and tactics and an existing or blank Position Description. *(You'll find a blank Position Description in the Appendix.)*

COMMUNICATING PLANNING INPUTS

What Will You Communicate?

Once you've considered your audience, you must create the appropriate message for your team meeting. This is the real *"essence"* of your presentation—the key element. Even though *"how"* you say something is important, if you have nothing to say, you'll be going nowhere fast.

Consider the following general agenda for your team meeting:

AGENDA

1. Introduce the Performance Management Cycle, including performance planning, as an ongoing organizational initiative

2. Explain the inputs you gathered in Step 1 (Incorporate Inputs Into The Individual Performance Plans)

3. Distribute the planning tools to the employees

4. Clarify your expectations for Step 3 of the Performance Planning Model (Draft Or Revise The Performance Plans)

Here is some additional information to support you on each agenda item:

---

1. Introduce the Performance Management Cycle, including performance planning, as an ongoing organizational initiative

---

You will begin the meeting by explaining how the three-phase Performance Management Cycle is being adopted by your organization in order to ensure both employee *and* organizational success. Let team members know that performance management is not an option, but a critical and visionary process to which your organization is committed.

COMMUNICATING PLANNING INPUTS

> 2. Explain the inputs you gathered in Step 1 (Incorporate Inputs Into The Individual Performance Plans)

Expand on the Planning Phase by discussing once again your organizational KRAs and KIs, work group KRAs and KIs, and the objectives and tactics that support them. Show your employees that they will be working together in support of the overall organization.

> 3. Distribute the planning tools to the employees

Create a packet for each employee prior to the team meeting. In addition to any handouts, this packet should contain:

> a. The Position Description for the individual's job family
> b. A Blank Performance Objectives Form
> c. A Blank Performance Action Plan Form

The forms you include may be ones that your organization has previously developed, your own new forms, or forms you're adopting from this guidebook *(see Appendix for samples)*.

Remember, now is not the time to discuss issues of compensation or any individual performance issues. In order to plan for peak performance, all that is necessary at this point is for each employee to understand and accept individual job responsibilities and how they link to work group objectives.

> 4. Clarify your expectations for Step 3 of the Performance Planning Model (Draft Or Revise The Performance Plans)

COMMUNICATING PLANNING INPUTS

Your team members may be expected to study the responsibilities outlined in their Position Descriptions, and to come up with at least three workable objectives. In addition, ask your team members to consider what they will need to reach their objectives (*e.g., learning new skills, etc.*).

Finally, you will end the meeting by setting up for the next step—drafting performance plans, which will take place in the next two or three weeks.

Overcoming Resistance

Some employees may be resistant to change, and might attempt to dismiss the importance of formulating goals and objectives. As a manager, you must firmly state your expectations in a clear and concise manner.

Nevertheless, while this is definitely serious stuff, don't cast yourself in the role of *"the enforcer."* Your goal at this point is to help your team members be motivated to fulfill your expectations, as well as those of the organization.

> ### At Jake's Market...
> P.J. and Milt prepared for the team meeting. Milt made sure there was plenty of bottled water on the table and that the candy bowl was full.
>
> *"This is the only reason I've been looking forward to the team meeting,"* Milt said, holding up a chocolate-covered mint and popping it into his mouth.
>
> P.J. rolled her eyes at him. *"I really want the employees to be as interested about the work group objectives and Position Descriptions as Terry and I are,"* she said. *"And I know a lot of it depends on how we present the material."*
>
> *"Okay, okay,"* Milt interjected. *"I'll do my best to try to get into this."*
>
> *"I hope so,"* Terry commented, *"because this meeting will set the stage for individual plans. We need you behind us."*

COMMUNICATING PLANNING INPUTS

As the employees entered the tiny conference room, they each picked up a packet of paper and settled in for the meeting. Bevy Klein read the meeting's "to-do" list. With her outgoing personality, management knew Bevy was already an asset to the store. *"I'm so glad we're covering how the teams work together,"* Bevy said. *"At Super Store, everyone had their own agenda. Sometimes it felt like we were working against each other."*

"This is a great time to work at Jake's, and I'm glad you're all here to learn how we're going to manage our performance better," Terry replied. *"Okay, let's start up the video and hear what Jake himself has to say."*

P.J. and Terry smiled as the group watched the video of the *"big boss"* talking about the future of Jake's, and how focusing on Key Result Areas would help ensure their success. Milt downed a few more chocolates. After the five-minute video was over, Terry said, *"Let's take a look at the phases in our Performance Management Cycle."* She walked over to a flip chart and explained the three phases diagrammed on the chart, pointing out how they were linked.

Also, she briefly explained a chart that outlined the various work group's KRAs, KIs, objectives, and tactics.

"Since we are starting with the Planning Phase, let's look at the Position Descriptions for each of your respective job families. We took a shot at revising them prior to this meeting, but feel free to let us know if we missed anything. After all, you do your job on a daily basis and know the ins and outs."

Terry gave the employees a little bit of time to look over the documents in their packets. P.J. watched their reactions.

"I do like the fact that we are planning rather than just reacting—that makes a lot of sense," said Clint, the most senior cashier and one who often questions new processes. Wisely, P.J. had previewed the meeting's agenda with Clint well beforehand. The management team knew that with Clint on their side, everyone would be more open to the changes.

"And Jake's does more than look at the bottom line," remarked José, one of the produce clerks at Jake's. *"Management knows I'm getting my college degree and need some flexibility, and they're always willing to work around my crazy schedule. I know clerks at other stores who don't have that."*

Terry began to describe the different forms in each employee's packet. Then she nudged Milt. He knew his role was to help the team understand the expectations of the management.

COMMUNICATING PLANNING INPUTS

> *"You all know I'm a simple man who likes simple words, so let me break this down further,"* Milt began. Then he moved to the flip chart and started to explain performance planning in nontechnical terms that every team member could understand. Terry smiled to herself. She could see that Milt was slowly coming around.
>
> When Milt was done, Terry checked her watch, then restated the expectations for the team: they were to review their job descriptions, and begin to list some personal objectives. *"Milt, P.J., and I will start setting times for the one-on-one meetings with each of you in the next two or three weeks.*

After The Meeting

Once your initial meeting is complete, your team members will have left the meeting with a packet containing the three key components of a performance plan—the tools to help them plan for success. They will also have gained some idea of how to use them.

Now you have set the stage for the next phase in the process—the actual drafting of individual performance plans. Since this is scheduled to occur in about two or three weeks, you and each team member should have adequate time to prepare your thoughts. In the meantime, relax, take a deep breath, and concentrate on thinking of projected objectives for each employee.

You can't over-think at this point. Don't limit yourself—let your mind be open to a wide variety of objectives. Make notes of your very best ideas and keep those notes handy. You will need them later.

CHAPTER FOUR WORKSHEET: PREPARING FOR YOUR TEAM MEETING

1. Think of one particular team that you will be addressing when you begin to initiate performance planning within your organization. List some possible presentation methods that will help communicate your message to this particular work group.

   _____
   _____
   _____
   _____
   _____
   _____
   _____
   _____

2. Prior to your meeting, complete the checklist to ensure that you are adequately prepared.

   ☐ Ideas for initial explanation of performance management:

   _____
   _____
   _____

COMMUNICATING PLANNING INPUTS

☐ Manner in which you will stress the importance of planning:

_____

_____

_____

_____

☐ Examples to be used to illustrate organizational KRAs and KIs, work group KRAs and KIs, and the objectives and tactics that support them. Who is responsible for preparing these?

_____ Overheads_____

_____ Slides _____

_____ Flip Charts_____

_____ Video/Computer_____

_____ Other _____

☐ Packets for each team member containing all tools required, as well as any handouts.

☐ Manner in which you plan to convey your expectations to the group:

_____

_____

☐ Ideas for summing up the meeting and setting the stage for drafting:

_____

_____

CHAPTER FIVE

THE POSITION DESCRIPTION

Based on the information in Chapter Four, you told your team members about the three tools needed to effectively plan for employee success *(Position Descriptions, Performance Objectives, and Performance Action Plans)*. Now it's time to tackle each one on an individual basis, in a one-on-one meeting, beginning with the Position Description.

The One-On-One Meeting

The work completed in this step—the drafting-and-revising step—may happen in a one-on-one meeting with you and each team member. After that, you will have time to think through the drafts before coming back together to finalize the performance plans.

❸ DRAFT OR REVISE PERFORMANCE PLANS

Drafting performance plans is a task requiring concentrated effort. Therefore, it is necessary to set aside an uninterrupted period of about two hours for each one-on-one drafting session.

The Importance Of The Position Description

Formulating high-quality Position Descriptions is a key step in performance planning. Position Descriptions are developed for job families. A job family is typically identified by the title of the job *(e.g., contract administrator, software engineer, cashier, etc.)*. This tool sets the groundwork for the other two components of the performance plan.

In the Position Description, you'll be defining the key responsibilities, the required skills, and the education and experience needed to perform well in the position. In addition, you'll be listing various measures and evaluations to gauge performance of these functions.

THE POSITION DESCRIPTION

Following are steps to draft or revise a description for a Procurement Specialist in a mid-sized organization. You can use this same process for the different job positions that report to you. Notice that on this form there are clear sections related to each element, as well as a method for indicating their relationships *(i.e., codes)*.

Each skill, measurement, and evaluation method is listed next to a generic code. These codes, which relate to each skill, measurement, and evaluation method, are then inserted in the appropriate column next to the responsibility they support. This is one method for showing relationships among the elements. It is better to do most of this matching in the final step when you have the entire description complete. However, you will find that some of this falls into place naturally as you complete each of the steps.

The purpose of the codes is to connect each responsibility with the means by which it will be assessed, *(i.e., needed skills, appropriate measurements, and evaluation methods)*. Coding is only one way of making this connection and is certainly *optional*. It proves to be an easy method for making the connections explicit without having to rewrite the same skill or measurement several times for each corresponding responsibility.

Whether you use a corporate-mandated form, or you have the freedom to create your own, you still may need to identify the elements listed here. So follow along as you learn to create a Position Description for a Procurement Specialist. When you create or revise the Position Descriptions for your own organization, you'll apply the steps you've learned and observed here.

THE POSITION DESCRIPTION

Before you begin to draft your Position Description, be sure to check with Human Resources to find out about any formal approval process that may be required to make changes to a Position Description. Typically, these are organization-specific, and exist to maintain consistency for positions, since employees with the same Position Description may actually reside in different departments within the same organization.

For example, each division may have an Administrative Support person. This job may have the same accountabilities in each division, to promote fairness in pay raises, etc., even though each administrative-support person's performance is probably evaluated by a different manager.

Drafting And Revising Your Position Description

Drafting Position Descriptions involves four steps. These steps include:

1. Identifying responsibilities and skills
2. Defining measures and evaluation methods
3. Determining education and experience needed
4. Matching codes to responsibilities

We'll proceed through these four steps in *"Building Block"* fashion, so you'll only be viewing the appropriate section(s) of the Position Description Form at each step.

Step 1: Identifying responsibilities and skills

Identifying the position's primary responsibilities and skills is the first step in filling out a Position Description. It's a logical place to start. Look at the responsibilities listed for the procurement specialist.

THE POSITION DESCRIPTION

This position is held accountable for seven primary responsibilities. Notice that each responsibility begins with an action word. Adding action words *(e.g., communicate, analyze, write, create, etc.)* makes it easier to list behaviors that can be measured.

RESPONSIBILITIES
1. Conduct Request For Proposals (RFPs)
2. Analyze supplier proposals
3. Prepare recommendations based on analysis of supplier proposals
4. Present recommendations to management
5. Assess supplier financial and operational capabilities
6. Negotiate contracts with suppliers
7. Create purchase orders using an on-line template

THE POSITION DESCRIPTION

For existing job descriptions, review the responsibilities and determine if they are still valid or need to be updated. For new positions, this is the place to start drafting. As you begin to fill out the primary responsibilities, ask the following questions:

---

1. What are the needs that are being filled by this position?

2. What are the types of projects or activities that the people filling this position will be working on?

3. What will be their primary accomplishments?

Using the *"80/20 Rule"* is a way to ensure that your list doesn't get overly fussy. Twenty percent of the responsibilities an employee handles may account for 80 percent of what they create. Strive to focus on key responsibilities, as well as required skills. Don't sweat the small stuff.

Using the answers to the questions in the box above, develop a list of seven to ten descriptive statements of the responsibilities and insert them in the spaces provided on the form.

If you get stuck, you will find a *"Position Description Thought Jogger"* in the Reference Material section of this guidebook to help you. Of course, this list is not exhaustive, and is intended to provide ideas to stimulate your thinking around those responsibilities you need to define.

Your next activity is to determine the types of skills needed to carry out those responsibilities.

THE POSITION DESCRIPTION

Like the responsibilities listed below, note that each skill begins with an action word *(see Reference Material section, "Position Description Thought Jogger")*.

RESPONSIBILITIES
1. Conduct Request For Proposals (RFPs)
2. Analyze supplier proposals
3. Prepare recommendations based on analysis of supplier proposals
4. Present recommendations to management
5. Assess supplier financial and operational capabilities
6. Negotiate contracts with suppliers
7. Create purchase orders using an on-line template

CODE	SKILLS (OBSERVABLE BEHAVIORS, NOT TRAITS/VALUES)
S1	Communicate and influence *(interpersonal, public presentations, etc.)*
S2	Analyze and interpret proposals and contracts
S3	Process data on computers *(mainframe, PC, word processor, and spreadsheet)*
S4	Write *(letters, memos, procurement contracts, etc.)*
S5	Organize workloads and prioritize competing objectives
S6	Interpret and present data
S7	Negotiate contracts *(compliance to standards, etc.)*
S8	Identify options and recommend courses of action

THE POSITION DESCRIPTION

The question to ask at this point is:

> *"What skills do these team members need at this point to successfully complete the listed responsibilities?"*

A common example involves the skills required to create a document on a PC. Such skills include the ability to type and the ability to create and save a document in a particular software package.

Less easily-quantified skills, like creativity and innovation, are more difficult to measure, but nonetheless may be required, and therefore, may be listed. The key is to focus on the essential five to eight skills, and don't try to list every possible skill imaginable. Otherwise, this step becomes an overwhelming task.

Step 2: Defining measures and evaluation methods

In this second step of drafting a Position Description, you will identify the five-to-eight potential measurements that will indicate overall performance for the position. Why so few? Because if you were to use every possible measure, a Position Description would resemble a small telephone book and tracking them would become your new avocation. You've got better things to do. In fact, over the course of a performance period, two or three of these measurements may very well *"rise to the top"* because they are the most important when it comes to defining success on the job. They will be used in discussions with your team members to improve and evaluate their performance. These measurements become the primary mechanisms in the upcoming phases of the Performance Management Cycle *(Coaching and Evaluating)*.

THE POSITION DESCRIPTION

Note that more than one measurement maybe related to each responsibility. This is typical. Most measurements will indicate performance in more than one area.

Think of the measurement as the type of information you need to collect to tell you how well an employee in this particular job is performing or carrying out the responsibilities.

Measurements can be difficult to define; and, if done poorly, can drive the wrong behavior. In the case where a sportswriter of a large newspaper is made directly responsible for the number of typographical errors in that section's ad copy, the wrong behavior could be prompted. You may find him spending too much time editing and not enough time writing.

RESPONSIBILITIES
1. Conduct Request For Proposals (RFPs)
2. Analyze supplier proposals
3. Prepare recommendations based on analysis of supplier proposals
4. Present recommendations to management
5. Assess supplier financial and operational capabilities
6. Negotiate contracts with suppliers
7. Create purchase orders using an on-line template

THE POSITION DESCRIPTION

CODE	SKILLS (OBSERVABLE BEHAVIORS, NOT TRAITS/VALUES)
S1	Communicate and influence (interpersonal, public presentations, etc.)
S2	Analyze and interpret proposals and contracts
S3	Process data on computers (mainframe, PC, word processor, and spreadsheet)
S4	Writing (letters, memos, procurement contracts, etc.)
S5	Organize workloads and prioritize competing objectives
S6	Interpret and present data
S7	Negotiate contracts (compliance to standards, etc.)
S8	Identify options and recommend courses of action

CODE	MEASUREMENTS	CODE	EVALUATION METHODS	EDUCATION/EXPERIENCE
M1	Customer satisfaction (ability to deal with others effectively, including suppliers)	E1		1.
M2	Accuracy (selecting relevant data; reaching accurate conclusions)	E2		2.
M3	Yield (throughput of purchase orders, contracts, complex negotiations, etc.)	E3		3.
M4	Clarity/conciseness (letters, memos, presentations, etc.)	E4		4.
M5	Organization (manage multiple tasks simultaneously)	E5		5.
M6	Quality (purchase orders, contracts, negotiations, and analyses, etc. are done right the first time)	E6		6.
M7		E7		7.
M8		E8		8.

PLANNING SUCCESSFUL EMPLOYEE PERFORMANCE

THE POSITION DESCRIPTION

On the other hand, if that same writer is held accountable for the accuracy of the article at the time it goes to press, he'll spend his time on more appropriate activities such as researching, interviewing, drafting, and ensuring that edited language does not alter the intent of the article, in addition to proofreading for typographical errors.

In this case, a good measurement of performance would be the *"percent of completely accurate articles that go to press."* Do you see how *"completely accurate"* contains a number of measurements for which the sportswriter should be held accountable?

Measurements are simply statements of the type of information you need to collect to indicate performance. Therefore, there must be a method for collecting that information. These *"evaluation methods"* should be inserted in the next column.

A major point to remember:

> *Don't throw away a good measurement because you can't immediately think of a way to collect the information!*

In the Procurement Specialist Position Description example, the *"E1 method"* (*feedback from clients, management, suppliers*) has never been used before in a formal way. But the supervisor realized that only through direct feedback could he get real data on each procurement specialist's performance in responsibility *"number 4"* (*present recommendations to management*) and responsibility *"number 6"* (*negotiate contracts with suppliers*).

Code	Evaluation Methods
E1	Feedback from clients, management, suppliers, etc., by teleconference or face-to-face interviews
E2	Direct observations and feedback from supervisor
E3	Review of output (e.g., RFPs) and coaching from supervisor

Even though the answer may not be obvious, and the system may not be in place, you can still come up with an answer. It just means you have your work cut out for you to establish the documentation, the collection tools, the tracking device, or whatever else you need to gather the needed data. Keep in mind that the *"80/20 Rule"* applies here as well, where 20 percent of your measurement data will probably provide you with 80 percent of what you need to know. Once again, refer to the *"Position Description Thought Jogger"* in the Reference Material section to assist you.

Step 3: Determining education and experience needed

You'll find that step three—determining the education and experience needed for each job position—is typically simpler than identifying responsibilities and measurements. Under *"education/ experience,"* list the *minimum* education required to carry out the job. This helps ensure that you don't choose someone who really shouldn't be in that position.

Consider including education/experience related to:

- Relevant and progressive job experience
- Demonstrated experiences *(provide examples of accomplishments, project plans, analyses, presentation materials, flowcharts, diagrams, etc.)*
- Academic course work or equivalent *(establish minimum qualifications by defining specific curriculum like "statistics" instead of "Business degree")*
- Relevant certifications, licenses, accreditations, credentials, etc.
- Relevant seminars, conferences, workshops, programs, etc.
- Special projects, experiences, etc.

THE POSITION DESCRIPTION

Refer to the Procurement Specialist position description section below. As you can see, this position needs both formal education and demonstrated experience to carry out the responsibilities listed. However, the numbers 2, 3, and 4 in the *"education/experience column"* will vary for an entry-level procurement Position Description. *(Remember: this description is for a Procurement Specialist.)* Many Position Descriptions will require differing types of education and experience, depending upon whether the position is entry-level or not.

EDUCATION/EXPERIENCE
1. College level courses or equivalent in Financial Analysis, Business Law, Price/Cost Analysis
2. Minimum of four years of direct purchasing experience in relevant commodities
3. Demonstrated experience in negotiating large-value contracts for goods/services
4. Demonstrated experience in coordinating intercompany acquisitions

Minimum requirements also apply to experience. Sometimes, experience is regulated by law, such as in cases where licensing is required. Other times, corporate policy and procedures dictate a certain number of years of experience. For example, your organization may desire management candidates to have at least five years of experience as a junior-level manager before they can be considered for senior management.

You must take into consideration your personal perspective. If you've discovered that staff members who have a minimum of two years of experience in a particular field are more successful, write it into your requirements.

The *"Education/Experience"* section of the Position Description is very helpful in determining employee development priorities, as well as career path planning, so pay close attention here.

THE POSITION DESCRIPTION

Step 4: Matching codes to responsibilities

In this final step, match the responsibilities with the three coded columns—skills, measurements, and evaluation methods.

Even though you may have determined much of this matching as you defined the different elements, it is important that you take one last look across the elements to determine relationships that weren't obvious before.

Ask yourself the following questions for each responsibility:

1. Which of the identified skills are critical to an individual's ability to perform the duties required?

2. Which of the measurements will provide information that suggests success (or failure) in performing those duties?

3. Which method(s) provide(s) the most efficient means to collect the information?

Fill in the code columns as appropriate, and your Position Description is complete!

THE POSITION DESCRIPTION

POSITION DESCRIPTION

JOB FAMILY/POSITION:	SALARY BAND:	DEPARTMENT:	ORIGINATED:	REVISED:
Procurement Specialist (Buyer)	Specialist/ Professional	Purchasing	6/1/XX	6/1/XX

RESPONSIBILITIES	SKILL CODES	MEASUREMENT CODES	EVALUATION METHOD CODES
1. Conduct Request For Proposals (RFPs)	S2, S3, S4, S5	M5	E3
2. Analyze supplier proposals	S2, S3, S5	M2, M5	E3
3. Prepare recommendations based on analysis of supplier proposals	S2, S3, S4, S5, S6, S8	M2, M4, M6	E1, E2, E3
4. Present recommendations to management	S1, S6, S8	M1, M2, M3, M4, M6	E3
5. Assess supplier financial and operational capabilities	S2, S3	M2, M3	E3
6. Negotiate contracts with suppliers	S1, S2, S5, S6, S7, S8	M1, M3, M5, M6	E1, E2
7. Create purchase orders using on-line template	S3, S4, S5	M2, M6	E3
8.			
9.			
10.			

THE POSITION DESCRIPTION

CODE	SKILLS (OBSERVABLE BEHAVIORS, NOT TRAITS/VALUES)
S1	Communicate and influence (interpersonal, public presentations, etc.)
S2	Analyze and interpret proposals and contracts
S3	Process data on computers (mainframe, PC, word processor, and spreadsheet)
S4	Writing (letters, memos, procurement contracts, etc.)
S5	Organize workloads and prioritize competing objectives
S6	Interpret and present data
S7	Negotiate contracts (compliance to standards, etc.)
S8	Identify options and recommend courses of action

CODE	MEASUREMENTS	CODE	EVALUATION METHODS	EDUCATION/EXPERIENCE
M1	Customer satisfaction (ability to deal with others effectively, including suppliers)	E1	Feedback from clients, management, suppliers, etc. by teleconference or face-to-face interviews	1. College level courses or equivalent in Financial Analysis, Business Law, Price/Cost Analysis
M2	Accuracy (selecting relevant data; reaching accurate conclusions)	E2	Direct observations and feedback from supervisor	2. Minimum of four years of direct purchasing experience in relevant commodities
M3	Yield (throughput of purchase orders, contracts, complex negotiations, etc.)	E3	Review of output (e.g., RFPs) and coaching from supervisor	3. Demonstrated experience in negotiating large-value contracts for goods/services
M4	Clarity/conciseness (letters, memos, presentations, etc.)	E4		4. Demonstrated experience in coordinating inter-company acquisitions
M5	Organization (manage multiple tasks simultaneously)	E5		5.
M6	Quality (purchase orders, contracts, negotiations, and analyses, etc. are done right the first time)	E6		6.
M7		E7		7.
M8		E8		8.

THE POSITION DESCRIPTION

At Jake's Market...

exactly one week after the team meeting, Terry's first one-on-one discussion with the cashiers began. She elected to start with Clint, a senior cashier and the team's resident skeptic.

"Thanks for your input on the Position Description form, Clint," Terry said as they reviewed the form. *"Let's start with the functions and responsibilities."*

Job Family/Position	Salary Band	Dept.
Cashier	Sr. Cashier	Cash/Wrap, #20

Functions and Responsibilities
1. Conduct customer checkout of merchandise
2. Verify and input new computer code numbers
3. Process cash, checks, credit, and refund orders
4. Maintain inventory data for case purchases
5. Maintain supplies at checkout counter
6. Supervise and assign baggers
7. Wrap/Bag orders

"One of the items missing on the old description was accessing the computer's inventory system and deducting case quantities," Clint remarked. *"So I added it. It's now number 4 on the list."*

"Good point," Terry replied. *"When customers buy a case or two of wine, it's essential to make that accurate inventory deduction. This is especially important during sales and the holidays."*

"I also added some skills to the list on the next page, Terry," Clint continued. *"With the addition of the scanners and debit-card transactions, the cashiers' jobs have changed."*

Terry read over the skills listed. She was pleased that Clint had added information. In doing so, he was *"buying into the program,"* and Terry knew this would connect him to the Performance Planning Model.

Skills
S1 - Communicate with customers, baggers, and staff
S2 - Use a scanner, debit card, cash register, and an inventory software program
S3 - Detect and remedy price or cash-register inaccuracies
S4 - Maintain supplies and troubleshoot equipment
S5 - Organize workload of baggers
S6 - Assist in receiving merchandise
S7 - Assist and substitute for manager in manager's absence

THE POSITION DESCRIPTION

> Terry flipped to her own Position Description that was also out on the table to double-check a point. *"I notice here in the skills section, Clint,"* Terry began, *"that you wrote that the cashier was to detect and remedy price or cash-register inaccuracies. You don't really need the skill (to remedy the inaccuracies) since only managers are allowed to manipulate pricing in the system."*
>
> Clint nodded in agreement. They made the change on the skills section and continued to review the measurements, evaluation methods, and education/experience categories.
>
> *"I'm still unclear on one part of the Measurement Section,"* Clint remarked after he and Terry had read over the complete Position Description for a Senior Cashier. He put an index finger on the item titled *"Customer Satisfaction."* *"How can one be effectively measured on the ability to deal with others? You're not going to make me count cheery smiles or force me to list how often I say 'Have a great day,' are you?"* Clint faked a giant frown.
>
> Terry smiled involuntarily. *"This may sound subjective, but it's not,"* she began. *"Think of customer satisfaction as a measurement that can be collected by feedback. The feedback comes from customers, other employees, and the management team. Customer satisfaction can be measured through our employee-of-the-month survey and through direct observation, and will indicate how well you are doing at your primary responsibility of 'conducting customer checkout of merchandise'."*
>
> Terry appreciated the points Clint raised. She gave him time to discuss concerns and other ideas before moving on with the meeting. The one-on-one meeting was going well, and Terry felt positive that drafting the Performance Objectives would also be successful.

Change is sometimes difficult for people to cope with. If you should find yourself or other team members resistant to taking this first step on the road to performance management, remember that it will all be worth it when your plan is carried out successfully.

Although it may seem to be a lot of work now, when things already appear to be running smoothly, do it anyway! Just as the longest journey begins with a single step, the formulation of your performance plan begins with initial acceptance of Position Descriptions.

THE POSITION DESCRIPTION

CHAPTER FIVE WORKSHEET: DRAFTING POSITION DESCRIPTIONS

1. List three to five primary responsibilities for a Job Family/Position at your organization.

   _____
   _____
   _____
   _____
   _____

2. Choose one of the responsibilities listed above and write it on the line below, and answer each of the questions below.

   Responsibility: _____

   a. What critical skills are needed to perform the responsibility?

   _____
   _____
   _____
   _____
   _____

THE POSITION DESCRIPTION

b. What measurement(s) would indicate successful performance of this responsibility?

_____
_____
_____
_____
_____

c. How would you collect this information *(i.e., evaluation method(s))*?

_____
_____
_____
_____
_____

3. Reproduce the Position Description form in the Appendix and create a Position Description for a team member who reports to you.

CHAPTER SIX

PERFORMANCE OBJECTIVES AND PERFORMANCE ACTION PLANS

You've already taken a good look at your employees' Position Descriptions and made necessary changes so that they more accurately reflect the job positions within your organization. Now you and your team members need to draft or revise their Performance Objectives and Performance Action Plans. You'll meet with each team member separately and begin with the Performance Objectives.

3. DRAFT OR REVISE PERFORMANCE PLANS

Defining Performance Objectives

Performance Objectives link individual performance with work group objectives and tactics. They are objective statements of conditions that will exist after work is performed that can be measured quantitatively. Performance Objectives are defined for individual team members, and describe specific outcomes for which they will be held accountable. The objectives clarify for the team members how they will contribute to team and organizational performance within the scope of their responsibilities as outlined in the Position Description.

Drafting Performance Objectives involves the following four steps:

1. Determine which work group objectives and tactics this individual will support
2. Define specific performance objectives
3. Consider all four types of objectives
4. Determine a target date for completion

PERFORMANCE ACTION PLANS

When drafting Performance Objectives, consider using only three to seven objectives for each of your direct reports. This is not to say that an employee will be limited to doing work only on these objectives over the course of the performance period. However, you will be responsible throughout Coaching and Evaluating to manage, monitor, support, and assess your employee's performance toward these objectives. It will be an impossible task to manage with a longer list.

Also, be aware that some of the objectives may already exist. Some project-related performance objectives may be multi-year, as long as progress can be evaluated on a fiscal year basis at key project milestones.

As you recall from chapter four, there should be a linkage from the top of the organization all the way down to individual Performance Objectives. Each team member's Performance Objectives should support the organization in its endeavors.

Also, in chapter five, you viewed the creation of a Position Description for a Procurement Specialist. Now meet John Jenkins, an experienced Procurement Specialist fulfilling those job responsibilities.

In John Jenkins' work group, an objective is to *"Increase the variety of vendors and suppliers by 20 percent by the second quarter,"* and some work group tactics to support it are *"to research and screen new vendor candidates"* and *"to develop a vendor certification program."*

The manager of the procurement department examined the Position Descriptions for the employees reporting to him. He decided that John Jenkins should become accountable for helping the work group to progress toward the objectives listed, since almost all of John's responsibilities outlined in the Position Description were related to managing supplier and vendor relations. During their one-on-one meeting, John and his manager drafted the following Performance Objectives:

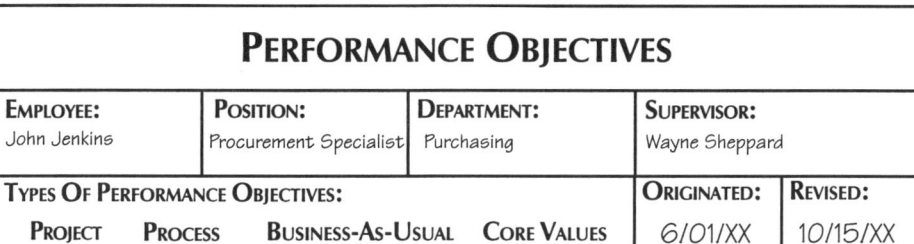

PERFORMANCE ACTION PLANS

PERFORMANCE OBJECTIVES

EMPLOYEE: John Jenkins	POSITION: Procurement Specialist	DEPARTMENT: Purchasing	SUPERVISOR: Wayne Sheppard	
TYPES OF PERFORMANCE OBJECTIVES: PROJECT PROCESS BUSINESS-AS-USUAL CORE VALUES			**ORIGINATED:** 6/01/XX	**REVISED:** 10/15/XX

OBJECTIVE	TYPE	TARGET DATE
To compile a potential new vendor pool.	Project	7/15/XX
To reduce the time to secure supplier contracts by fifteen percent.	Process	3/15/XX
To ensure that all suppliers meet vendor certification criteria 100 percent of the time.	Business-As-Usual	4/1/XX
To demonstrate respect for individual differences of other team members.	Core Values	on-going

EMPLOYEE SIGNATURE: *John Jenkins* **DATE:** 10/15/XX

SUPERVISOR SIGNATURE: *Wayne Sheppard* **DATE:** 10/15/XX

PERFORMANCE ACTION PLANS

To be complete, an objective must include the following:

- An action word *(what you want to accomplish)*
- The end result *(described by a performance target)*
- A time element *(indicates anticipated completion date)*

Take the project objective as an example. The objective reads: *"To compile a potential new vendor pool by 7/15/XX."*

Action word = compile
End result = potential new vendor pool
Time element = by 7/15/XX

The word *"potential"* is important. It indicates that the pool would not necessarily have to be finalized at this point, but an acceptable outcome is a *"suggested"* pool of vendors.

Types Of Performance Objectives

Did you notice in the Performance Objective sample form that there are four types of objectives? You should consider all four types when writing Performance Objectives with each team member during your individual meetings.

They include the following:

The Four Types Of Performance Objectives
- Project
- Process
- Business-As-Usual
- Core Values

"Project" objectives

Many team members may have objectives that describe specific projects they are responsible to complete over a period of time. A project can be defined as *"a specific, goal-directed, time-bound undertaking requiring the commitment of varied skills and resources."*

For example, look at the following two *"project"* objectives:

> **PROJECT**
>
> ♦ To create the high-level design for conflict-resolution training by 10/15/XX.
>
> ♦ To develop the new client contact file by 3/1/XX.

"Process" objectives

"Process" objectives are those which describe the intention to improve a job process, such as streamlining a series of activities that individuals go through to accomplish certain job tasks. Look at the following two examples of *"process"* objectives:

> **PROCESS**
>
> ♦ To streamline the customer/interview process from ten minutes to six minutes by 8/1/XX.
>
> ♦ To improve the material-design process to ensure hand-off to shipping on schedule 100 percent of the time by 11/1/XX.

"Business-as-usual" objectives

"Business-as-usual" objectives relate to regular, everyday job performance, and how that performance might be improved. They highlight ongoing assignments that are value-added and necessary.

Consider the following two examples of *"business-as-usual"* objectives:

BUSINESS-AS-USUAL

- To learn a graphics-design tool to create multi-colored presentation visuals by 7/10/XX.
- To increase the average monthly number of sales calls by 20 percent by 2/14/XX.

"Core values" objectives

Core values are the underlying guiding principles your organization deems important and those it wishes to operate within. As a rule, Performance Objectives that support core values will be more internally focused. Ideally, the theme of core values should run through each objective.

Read the following two examples of *"core values"* objectives:

CORE VALUES

- To demonstrate a focus on *"continuous improvement"* by actively participating on at least two process improvement teams by year's end.
- To demonstrate that *"customers come first"* by responding to all customer calls within ten minutes of receipt on my pager.

Take some time to consider each team member's perspective as you develop the Performance Objectives. Throw out the *"cookie cutter"* mentality and strive to uncover which objectives are most appropriate for each member. You may need to develop about three to seven objectives for each team member, so choose carefully.

PERFORMANCE ACTION PLANS

"Performance Objectives" are often *"stretch"* and *"developmental"* objectives. Stretch objectives refer to projects that associates complete in addition to their regular job responsibilities, while developmental ones often provide complex, new challenges.

As Position Descriptions become available, consider adding the following introductory paragraph above the list of *"Performance Objectives"* for each associate:

- *"In addition to completing all responsibilities as defined and measured on the attached Position Description, this associate will ..."* (followed by the Performance Objectives).

Terry and Clint continued...

their meeting, each taking time to communicate clearly. *"With the overall work group objective of reducing checkout time, we are directly supporting headquarters,"* she stated.

"As I understand it, to fulfill that objective, we need to streamline the checkout process. The merchandise scanners will cut seconds off the process, but the cashiers need to be trained on how to use them efficiently," Clint stated.

"You're right," Terry began, *"but in-store training will take care of that. In order to support this changeover, I'd like to have you become our resident expert in the use of the system. Can we agree that one of your Performance Objectives will be to become the lead on transitioning to scanners in the store by mid year?"*

"I like that idea," responded Clint. *"On the Performance Action Plan, let's add that I'll be going to the training workshop and reading additional stuff on the scanners."*

"Whoa! Slow down," Terry interjected. *"Let's finish defining your objectives first and then move on to the actions to support them."* She knew that Clint knew his job and how to effectively fulfill the job requirements better than anyone else. *"What else slows down the checkout process other than the inability to scan?"* Terry asked.

"We spend way too much time on returns, refunds, and dealing with customer concerns," Clint answered.

"If that's the case," Terry said, *"How might you contribute in that area over the next year?"*

Terry and Clint continued their discussions until he had five Performance Objectives which they both felt would make him directly contribute to work group and organization-wide success....

PERFORMANCE ACTION PLANS

When formulating your employees' Performance Objectives, you may choose to reproduce the Performance Objectives form you'll find in the Appendix. Do remember, however, that you don't have to use this exact format to achieve peak results. Just make sure that whatever form you use contains room for several Performance Objectives and their target-completion dates. In addition, when you and each team member come to a final agreement in the next step, you will both sign the form, so make sure there's room for signatures.

Drafting Your Performance Action Plans

The final component of performance plans is the Performance Action Plan, which helps team members delineate key actions and milestones, deliverables and results, key resources required, and potential risks. Performance Action Plans are most useful when fleshing out complex Performance Objectives, even though they can be used to describe the actions to accomplish any objective. This component can be initiated at anytime during the year or at anytime during a project.

You will want to use Performance Action Plans in any of the following circumstances:

a. Any affected party, *(e.g. manager, team member, senior manager, customer, supplier)* is unsure about how to approach achieving an objective. This process will help prompt a discussion and gain agreement on key actions, expectations, and concerns.

b. One of the Performance Objectives is viewed as highly complex, vague, critical, politically sensitive, or resource-intensive. This process will ensure the proper attention to deliverables and results.

c. The team member, manager, or work group has not achieved past Performance Objectives. Note: Using this supplemental worksheet does not necessarily suggest the associate, manager, or work group *"performed"* in an undesirable way. It could be that the performance expectations were unclear and the unaccountable party got blamed.

PERFORMANCE ACTION PLANS

Since there may not be ample time during your two-hour, one-on-one drafting session to complete the Performance Action Plans for every objective that needs them, you should stress the *"how-to's"* of drafting a Performance Action Plan. Then, at the end of the meeting, ask the team member to prepare Action Plans and submit them at a later date.

Take a brief look at the example of a Performance Action Plan on page 75. You may choose to include all of the elements shown, or you may choose to alter your actual form to include different elements to better meet your organization's needs. At a minimum, complete the following steps:

♦ List the individual Performance Objective at the top of the sheet

♦ Determine actions and/or milestones for that objective

♦ Describe what needs to be delivered (the results) for each action

♦ List the required resources for each action

---

1. List the individual Performance Objective

Let's say that the senior sales staff member of an electronics firm is drafting Performance Action Plans with an executive-level Administrative Assistant, who is part of the sales presentation team. One of the work group objectives is *"to streamline the sales meeting presentation process,"* and the assistant's individual Performance Objective is *"to develop the capability to produce effective overheads, slides, and computerized slide shows for the sales meetings."* If you were the Administrative Assistant, you would begin drafting your Action Plan by listing this Performance Objective at the top of the page.

2. Determine actions for the objective

Next, you have to determine those actions that must occur in order to achieve the Performance Objective you have chosen. These actions should be measurable, and should outline the critical and essential project steps, even if you will need to attach additional pages. In this case, both the supervisor and Assistant may determine that the Assistant needs to obtain and learn a new software program in order to generate high-tech slides and graphics.

3. Describe what needs to be delivered (the results) for each action

In this step, you'll list the expected, measurable results of each action. This is important to help clarify expectations for desired performance *(and evaluate successful or unsuccessful performance)*. Try to be as complete as possible, including both the obvious and less obvious expected results for the actions defined in our Administrative Assistant example. A deliverable *(or result)* of learning the new computer program is that the Assistant should be able to create slides and graphics with the new software within the next two months. Including the time factor in this section provides for accountability.

4. List the required resources for each action

Now, you'll need to determine the required resources to carry out the actions. By listing those resources which are considered substantial, essential, or worthy of attention, you avoid the possibility of overlooking critical *"puzzle pieces"* required for success. Examples of this type of resource could be large budget items required to complete the project, or a person with a special expertise who does not report to you.

Continuing the Administrative Assistant example, the Assistant will need a budget to purchase the software program described above, as well as pay for a software training class.

PERFORMANCE ACTION PLAN

EMPLOYEE: John Jenkins	POSITION: Procurement Specialist	DEPARTMENT: Purchasing	SUPERVISOR: Wayne Sheppard	
PERFORMANCE OBJECTIVE: To compile a potential new vendor pool.			**ORIGINATED:** 6/15/XX	**REVISED:** 6/15/XX

ACTIONS/MILESTONES	DELIVERABLES/RESULTS	REQUIRED RESOURCES
1. Conduct external search	Documented summaries of potential vendors by February	Staff member support for Survey development (10 hrs) Text processing (5 hrs) Data analysis (5 hrs)
2. Benchmark competitor product/vendors	Analyzed results comparisons by 4/1/xx	Consultant resources for benchmark study ($20k)
3. Issue requests for vendor information and review	Recommendations in database by July	Text processing support (10 hrs)
4. Establish a potential pool	Pool description and certification process by September	Contact with Management-level decision team

RISKS, IMPACTS, AND LIKELIHOOD (High, Medium, Low) | OPTIONS AND RECOMMENDATIONS

RISK: Changing priorities (i.e., pulled off the project to work on something else)
IMPACTS: Loss of momentum and experience (others need more time to ramp up)
LIKELIHOOD: Medium

- Obtain internal/external resources to help
- Provide cost/benefit analysis to boss "on the fly"
- Say "no" to changing priorities

RISK: Can't reach a consensus on best applicants
IMPACTS: Possible delays, dissension, missed opportunities
LIKELIHOOD: Low

- Obtain objectives review by external consultant
- Establish decision-making process to break ties for consensus
- Live with a majority vote

RISK: Vendors won't pass certification requirements
IMPACTS: Small pool which cannot meet our needs
LIKELIHOOD: Medium

- Lessen requirements
- Continue search
- Support vendor to achieve certification

Optional steps

Because it's not a perfect *(or stable)* world, you may not be able to meet all the objectives you plan for. This is where the final two elements come into the picture. You must plan for the unexpected. The final two elements are *"Risks, Impacts, and Likelihood"* and *"Options and Recommendations."*

"Risks, Impacts And Likelihood," is optional. It is included to encourage the manager and team member to challenge and revise their *"Actions/Milestones"* above. The primary objective of the discussion is to reduce anticipated challenges by taking proactive steps.

Users will find this section expanding during the first draft and reducing by the second draft as the *"Options And Recommendations"* are built-in to improve the *"Actions/Milestones"* above. The final draft should have the fewest challenges possible that must be managed through contingency plans.

"Risks, Impacts And Likelihood" can pertain to the entire *"Performance Objective,"* any key *"Actions/Milestones," "Deliverables/Results,"* or *"Required Resources."* For *"Likelihood,"* use *"High"* (greater than 66 percent), *"Medium"* (greater than 33 percent), or *"Low"* (less than 33 percent). *"Low"* probability challenges are worth noting if the *"Impacts"* are critical.

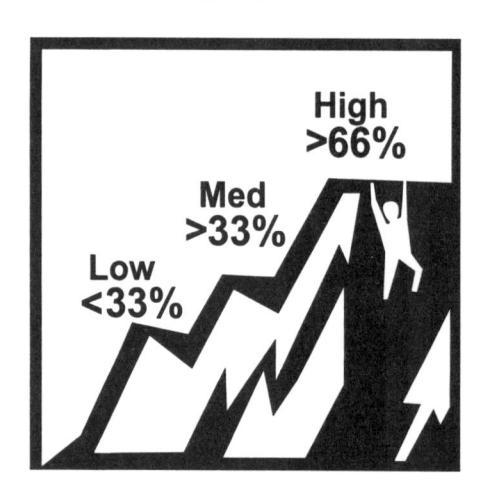

To define the risks, impacts and likelihood, you must ask yourself the following questions:

> **Risks:**
> What could possibly change or go wrong? What might contribute to not accomplishing the actions in this plan?
>
> **Impacts:**
> If the change or risk occurs, how will this plan be affected? What might happen as a result?
>
> **Likelihood:**
> What is the probability of the change or risk happening? Is it high, medium, or low?

"Options And Recommendations" should be more proactive (*i.e., used to add critical steps to "Actions/Milestones"*) than reactive (*i.e., contingency plans*). At a minimum, options should be generated for those medium and high-probability changes or risks, and at least one should be highlighted as the recommended approach. Developing a list of options and recommendations is a proactive way to deal with challenges. It will help you to anticipate changes and risks, and allow for success by having a plan in place prior to the actual disruption, when discouragement or panic might otherwise occur.

By taking the time to list the options, you are taking a proactive rather than reactive view of the project. In fact, this listing will help you to identify those team members who believe they are not able to take steps to overcome barriers to implementation, resulting in opportunities for you to coach them in their development of good judgement, analysis, and assessment skills.

PERFORMANCE ACTION PLANS

Options are alternative actions—not the ones listed under the "*Actions/Milestones*" column. Sometimes it requires out-of-the-box thinking to come up with a way to get around the unexpected, and this type of thinking can be quite challenging.

RISKS, IMPACTS AND LIKELIHOOD (HIGH, MEDIUM, LOW)	OPTIONS AND RECOMMENDATIONS
RISK: Vendors won't pass certification requirements **IMPACTS:** Small pool that cannot meet our needs **LIKELIHOOD:** Medium	Lessen requirements Continue search Support vendor to achieve certification

Other times it is simply a matter of thinking through the possibilities ahead of time.

RISKS, IMPACTS AND LIKELIHOOD (HIGH, MEDIUM, LOW)	OPTIONS AND RECOMMENDATIONS
RISK: Can't reach a consensus on best applicants **IMPACTS:** Possible delays, dissension, missed opportunities **LIKELIHOOD:** Low	Obtain objective review by external consultant Establish decision-making process to break ties for consensus Live with a majority vote

Before the meeting ends, schedule another follow-up meeting to finalize the plan. Give your team members ample opportunity to complete the Action Plans, as some data-gathering may be required (*e.g., checking prices and availability of new equipment, cost of staff support time, etc.*). Plan on allowing two-to-three weeks to fully prepare.

PERFORMANCE ACTION PLANS

Terry and Clint returned to the office...

after a short break. Terry's performance plan included an objective to have her staff become familiar with 95 percent of the store's products by year's end. *"Have you tried these new freeze-dried Apple Crispies?"* Terry asked, offering Clint the bag of crispy, spicy-flavored fruit. Clint shook his head, and Terry remarked, *"How can the team tell customers about the products, if they've never tasted them?"*

Clint smiled, then took a chip and started to write some actions in the Performance Action Plan. Then he stopped. *"I'm puzzled with this format, Terry."*

"No problem. Let's take one objective and break it down." Terry wrote one Performance Objective at the top of a sheet. It was: To be the store's scanner expert by the year's end. *"To achieve this objective,"* Terry said, *"you'll want to list actions, how the outcomes of those actions can be measured, and other items pertaining to the action."*

"Okay," Clint said. *"To achieve the objective, I'll learn how to use and be comfortable with the system, including the store's scanning software, by the last week in October. Then, in the first week of November, I'll take that workshop on the system. By the middle of November, I will have spent at least two hours with everyone on the cashier team to instruct them on the finer points of the system. As an ongoing action, I'll be available to resolve problems. I'll be a resource."*

Terry watched as Clint jotted notes on the Action Plan. *"Your next step,"* she reminded him, *"is to finalize the other objectives in this same way."*

As Clint left, taking the *"Apple Crispies"* with him, Terry knew that performance planning was working. In about two weeks, she'd again meet with Clint as well as everyone individually on the staff, to finalize their performance plans.

Are you ready to take it to the next level? You'll soon be entering the negotiation phase where these drafts will be finalized by you and your team member. Be sure to polish those effective management and coaching skills. They'll come in handy as you put a cap on the development of the individual performance plan.

CHAPTER SIX WORKSHEET: PERFORMANCE OBJECTIVES AND PERFORMANCE ACTION PLANS

1. Consider the four types of Performance Objectives *(project, process, business-as-usual, and core values)*. Using yourself or one of your team members as an example, list a sample of each type:

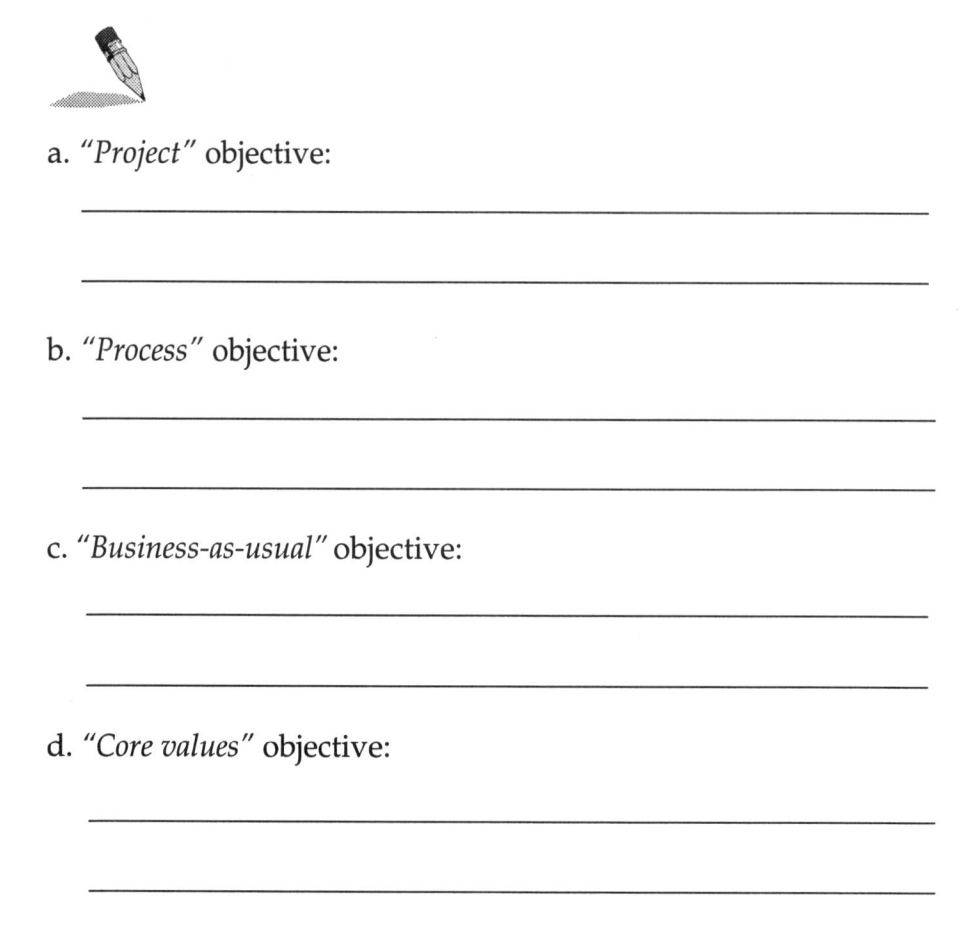

   a. *"Project"* objective:
   _____
   _____

   b. *"Process"* objective:
   _____
   _____

   c. *"Business-as-usual"* objective:
   _____
   _____

   d. *"Core values"* objective:
   _____
   _____

2. Choose one Performance Objective from Question #1 and, using the form on the following page, draft a Performance Action Plan for that objective.

PERFORMANCE ACTION PLANS

PERFORMANCE ACTION PLAN

EMPLOYEE:	POSITION:	DEPARTMENT:	SUPERVISOR:

PERFORMANCE OBJECTIVE:	ORIGINATED:	REVISED:

ACTIONS/MILESTONES	DELIVERABLES/RESULTS	REQUIRED RESOURCES
1.		
2.		
3.		
4.		

RISKS, IMPACTS AND LIKELIHOOD (HIGH, MEDIUM, LOW)	OPTIONS AND RECOMMENDATIONS
RISK: IMPACTS: LIKELIHOOD:	
RISK: IMPACTS: LIKELIHOOD:	
RISK: IMPACTS: LIKELIHOOD:	

CHAPTER SEVEN

FINALIZING THE PERFORMANCE PLAN

Once the overall package of Position Description, Performance Objectives, and Performance Action Plans is finalized, it becomes the blueprint from which each employee will be working. Therefore, it should be treated as a negotiated agreement.

4 — FINALIZE THE PERFORMANCE PLANS

The performance plan serves as a key element in all three phases of the Performance Management Cycle—Planning, Coaching, and Evaluating. It will be up to you as team leader to coach your team members through the effective implementation of their plans. Eventually, the finalized plan will include the measures by which each team member's performance is evaluated.

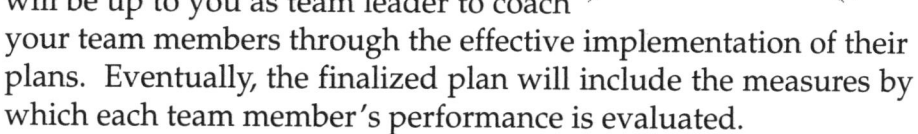

Continuous Planning / Coaching / Learning / Evaluating — Measurement

FINALIZING THE PERFORMANCE PLAN

Where You Should Be

As you approach the final step of the Planning Phase, a number of milestones are behind you. Take a moment to double check that you have carried out the following key elements before you finalize the plan:

- ☑ You have completed (or updated) the Position Description

- ☑ You have contacted Human Resources and checked into any concerns in regard to Position Description changes and potential reclassification of employees

- ☑ Together, you and each team member have drafted a set of Performance Objectives that support organizational and work group KRAs and KIs, objectives, and tactics

- ☑ Each team member has formulated Action Plans; and, depending upon the amount of research this entails, you have decided to either finalize immediately or meet in two-to-three weeks to finalize

As you begin to finalize your team members' plans, your time and effort will be spent in negotiation and interpersonal employee relations. Before you begin sharpening those negotiation skills, however, it is critical that you look at what you need to accomplish.

FINALIZING THE PERFORMANCE PLAN

Finalizing The Plan

First, you'll want to ensure that the plan is workable *(therefore, adjust where necessary)*; and second, you'll need to get the Performance Objectives form signed and in place. This may sound simple, but without two signatures on the line, you don't have an agreement.

> ### *Two weeks later,...*
> all three store managers—Terry, Milt, and P.J.—met to review the status of the performance plans. Terry asked, *"Ready to look over all we've accomplished?"*
>
> *"We have completed Position Description changes and have checked for any concerns regarding reclassification,"* P.J. piped in.
>
> *"And we've met one-on-one with all our team members. They certainly brought up great ideas,"* remarked Milt.
>
> P.J. picked it up with, *"Also, each employee has a set of Performance Objectives that work for all of us and support the KRAs and KIs."*
>
> *"To be truthful,"* Milt admitted, *"I didn't believe all this could be possible."*
>
> *"We know you didn't,"* replied Terry and P.J. in unison and then smiled knowingly at Milt. *"But the work isn't entirely over,"* Terry cautioned. *"Bevy has concerns about her Action Plan. We're meeting at four to talk about it."*
>
> As Terry finished the meeting with her assistant managers, she thought about the upcoming meeting. Bevy's work was typically excellent and error free, and she had initiative. Terry was concerned that the newest cashier might be dissatisfied at Jake's or with the performance-planning process. The young woman had refrained from signing her performance plan for three days. Why? Terry was eager to resolve the problem....

FINALIZING THE PERFORMANCE PLAN

Preparing To Negotiate

Not only do you need to approach these final meetings with extreme respect for all team members and their goals, but you, as manager, must actively represent the overall organizational objectives. How smoothly the negotiation process goes is largely up to you. However, do make sure that you consider each individual team member's opinion. This plan is going to affect the team member's work life *(and probably your own)* on a day-to-day basis.

If a simple run-through of each item yields mutual agreement on each point, you're done! Go ahead and sign the plan. It is now your performance contract.

If your situation isn't quite so neat, don't despair. Confront each difference of opinion by tracing each aspect of the Performance Objective or Action Plan directly back to the original work group or organizational KRA that prompted it.

Show the team member how each objective fits into the overall scheme and stress just why you feel it is important to the organization. If necessary, go down the *"laundry list"* of potential benefits. Include not only the fit of the objective or plan to the big picture, but also:

- The importance of the objective to the team member's personal career development *(e.g., learning new skills or participating in new programs)*. Not only will this make the team member fit better within the organization, but he will also gain skills to become more marketable within the field in general.

- The importance of the objective to the success of the organization *(e.g., if jobs aren't completed on time and the organization fails, jobs may be cut)*. Again, reiterate not only the *"way"* the performance plan is linked to the overall plan, but *"how"* the success or failure of each contribution affects the bottom line.

FINALIZING THE PERFORMANCE PLAN

- The importance of the objective to the satisfaction of the customer or client *(e.g., customers will respond to positive changes with increased business)*. When formulating inputs into the plan, you assessed customer requirements and the market in general. Striving to meet the needs of your customers is now built into your plan.

While you'll be highlighting the positive outcomes should the plan succeed, you'll also need to cover the downside of what can happen if a team member does not comply with the plan. However, don't concentrate on the negative aspects of non-compliance, as this can be an overt job threat, and may force the team member to cooperate strictly out of concern for his position. Try not to make the agreement a *"do or die"* proposition.

Should you still face challenges in seeing eye-to-eye, revert to basic negotiation skills. Rephrasing the same content in a different way may help to clarify ideas on which you both basically agree. People often get stuck on a certain word or phrase that keeps them from understanding the true message.

Some challenges you face may be caused by:

- Lack of interest in the overall Performance Management Cycle
- Peer perception (e.g., how a possible change of status will be seen by other team members)
- Interpersonal conflicts (e.g., underlying conflicts between the team member and manager)
- A different vision or view of the position
- Home/personal needs
- Resistance to change
- Lack of motivation
- Fear of failure
- Compensation issues

FINALIZING THE PERFORMANCE PLAN

Nevertheless, as you enter your meeting with each individual team member, remember these factors:

- Continually focus on the linkages between the Performance Objectives, and the organizational and work group KRAs and KIs

- Be as well-informed as possible before entering into negotiation

- Identify beforehand those objectives that are vital to you and the organization, and those with which you are flexible

- Stick to the issues and avoid becoming bogged down in insignificant details

- Be aware of your team member's desired outcome

- Ask questions to clarify your team member's viewpoint and ask for a response to your viewpoint

- If negotiations hit a snag, know when to break and regroup

FINALIZING THE PERFORMANCE PLAN

When Bevy refused a frosty Kahala Iced Koffee,...

a new line of bottled drinks that all regional stores were featuring, Terry knew something was wrong. Bevy usually delighted in sampling all the merchandise.

"I'm really nervous even talking about this. I can't even force myself to sign the performance plan," Bevy started. Her words came out in a rush, but she continued before Terry could even try to ease her fears. *"I've been happy here the last two months, but with the new plan, that's all going to change."*

Terry knew she had to handle the situation carefully. *"I'm glad you've come in to talk with me, Bevy. That's what this stage in the program is all about."*

Bevy took a deep breath. *"Remember how I told you at Super Store that after just three months I was promoted to senior cashier? Well, the other cashiers were resentful and said hurtful things. I'm the youngest here, again, yet I want to become a senior cashier, then assistant manager, and ultimately work into becoming a manager like you, Terry. I'd like to use my brand new business degree. I know we talked about these goals two weeks ago. Now, seeing them on paper, I'm reminded of the incident at Super Store and I'm not comfortable."* She started to reach for a Kahala Koffee and then stopped.

Terry tried not to sigh aloud. She knew this challenge wouldn't be too tough, as long as she carefully chose her words. *"Bevy,"* Terry began, *"every team member in the store has specific goals. Action Plans are formatted to take into consideration individual aspirations. For example, on my own Action Plan, I've outlined the steps to move into regional management. I love the stores, but I need to stretch. I need challenges. One of the stock clerks has her eye on becoming a cashier. One of the baggers is determined to become a stock clerk. Regardless of what happened at Super Store, with the Performance Management Cycle, each of us at Jake's is in charge of our own future. You chart your individual course for success, and we'll deal with the obstacles, including other people's behavior, as they come up."*

Bevy thought for a moment, then pulled the performance plan across the desk. She signed it, smiled, and grabbed a bottle of iced coffee. *"Making the move to Jake's was the best thing I've ever done."*

Watching the energetic cashier leave her office, Terry knew that future negotiations might not go as easily. Yet, for now, she felt lucky, and was convinced that performance planning was going to make a big difference at Jake's Market.

It is vital that you and your team member at least reach a compromise on each point before you finalize the plan. Agreeing to disagree will not work. Should things get really heated, back off, take a break, and reschedule the meeting.

FINALIZING THE PERFORMANCE PLAN

Do keep in mind, however, that you won't have much more time for revision. You'll soon be entering the Coaching Phase of the Performance Management Cycle, in which these actual plans will be carried out. The finalized performance plan will be the agreement to carry you into it.

Nevertheless, in the real world, changes in Performance Objectives and Performance Action Plans may occur frequently. Computerizing these plans makes them easier to update as needed. Just be sure that previous plans and decisions may be reviewed when needed.

The Performance Plan As An Agreement

Once you have finalized performance plans with each team member, start thinking about the important ways this plan will help you in the Evaluating Phase. Each performance plan now forms the basis for decisions that affect compensation and promotions. In turn, it could also lead to employee demotion or reclassification.

Each performance plan includes the objectives that you will be monitoring throughout the year. And, since you've added measurable objectives, monitoring and evaluating performance is much easier. If you've done a thorough job, each performance plan will allow you to collect real data on which to base decisions when it comes time to evaluate.

In the Coaching Phase of the Performance Management Cycle, you will learn how to create *"document files"* to log the data throughout the year. This data will include direct observations you have made throughout the year of the employee's performance on the job. You will learn just how to deal with the challenges that can plague day-to-day operations. Through effective coaching, you will not only manage these challenges, but set higher goals for success and achievement. This process is covered in detail within the practical guidebook, *Coaching For Peak Employee Performance*, published by Richard Chang Associates, Inc.

Eventually, when the time comes to enter the Evaluation Phase of the Performance Management Cycle, your team should be performing not only up to par, but above!

FINALIZING THE PERFORMANCE PLAN

CHAPTER SEVEN WORKSHEET: FINALIZING YOUR PERFORMANCE PLANS

1. Take a look at some Performance Objectives you have written for an individual employee and identify those you feel will need Action Plans. Choose two of these objectives, and explain why a detailed Action Plan is required.

   Objective # 1:
   _____
   _____

   Reason(s):
   _____
   _____
   _____
   _____

   Objective # 2:
   _____
   _____

   Reason(s):
   _____
   _____
   _____
   _____

FINALIZING THE PERFORMANCE PLAN

2. Keeping your work group in mind, think of some conflicts or objections that might arise during the course of finalizing your plans, and how you might overcome these situations.

Conflict/Objection	Ways To Overcome
1.	
2.	
3.	
4.	

FINALIZING THE PERFORMANCE PLAN

3. What, in your opinion, are the reasons for signing the performance plan and making it a formal agreement?

_____
_____
_____
_____
_____
_____
_____
_____
_____
_____

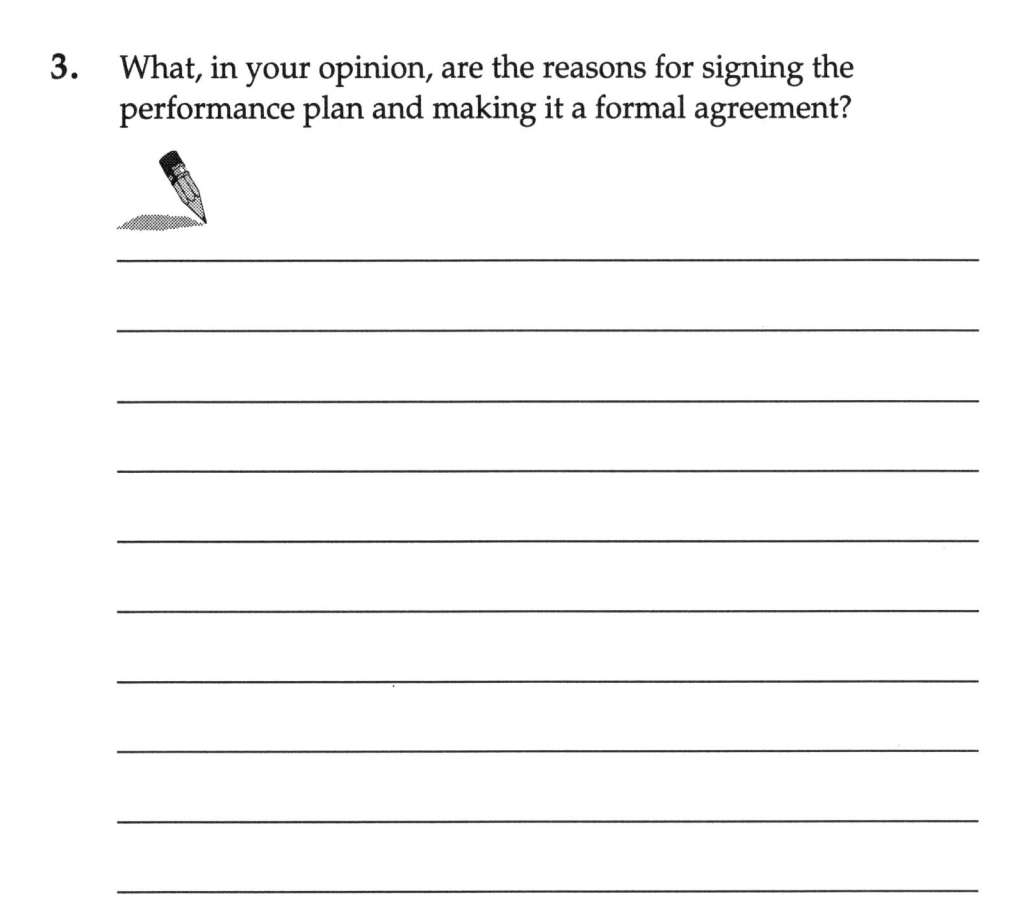

4. (Optional activity) If you feel comfortable doing so, share your list of possible conflicts with a suitable partner and actually role play what you would say to the team member during the negotiation process.

CHAPTER EIGHT

SUMMARY

You and your organization have made the decision to plan for successful employee performance. It's an important decision, one that will definitely impact your organization.

Maybe *"performance management"* is new to you. It could also be that you had no idea of what a Key Result Area was before you opened this guidebook. However, you've now set your sights on some KRAs that impact your work group, and every team member is aware of *(and plans to work towards)* achieving success in those critical areas.

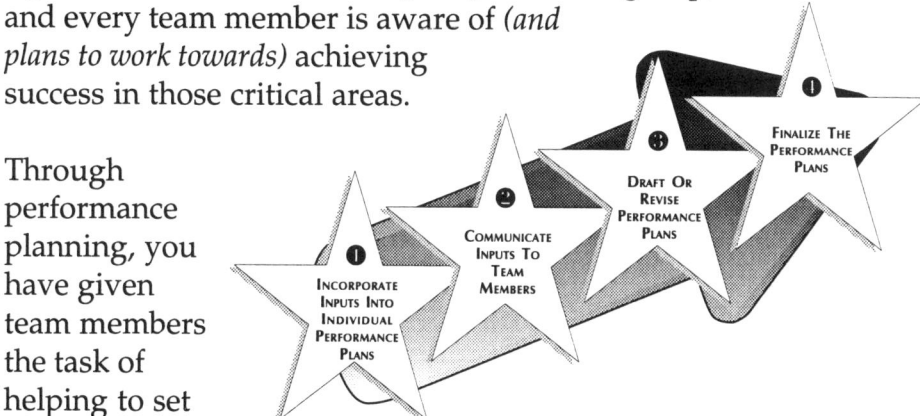

Through performance planning, you have given team members the task of helping to set their own goals and objectives, directly linked to those of the organization. In essence, performance planning requires each employee to become a more focused, integral member of the organization.

① INCORPORATE INPUTS INTO INDIVIDUAL PERFORMANCE PLANS
② COMMUNICATE INPUTS TO TEAM MEMBERS
③ DRAFT OR REVISE PERFORMANCE PLANS
④ FINALIZE THE PERFORMANCE PLANS

Through performance management, each and every team member will begin to work smarter and in complete coordination with the organization as a whole.

Begin now. Coordinate with your team members to get those performance plans signed and in place. Spending the time and effort it takes to get a truly effective performance plan in place will pay off in the future.

Don't sell yourself short. Even if you break a sweat climbing this initial performance-management *"hill,"* you'll be coasting by the time you enter the next two phases. It all begins with a plan.

APPENDIX

REFERENCE MATERIAL

The Position Description 98

Performance Objectives 100

Performance Action Plan 101

Position Description Thought Jogger:
    Responsibilities 102
    Skills 103
    Measurements 104
    Evaluation Methods and Education/Experience 105

Pages 98-101 in the Appendix are provided for you to photocopy and use appropriately.

APPENDIX

POSITION DESCRIPTION				
JOB FAMILY/POSITION:	SALARY BAND:	DEPARTMENT:	ORIGINATED:	REVISED:
RESPONSIBILITIES		SKILL CODES	MEASUREMENT CODES	EVALUATION METHOD CODES
1.				
2.				
3.				
4.				
5.				
6.				
7.				
8.				
9.				
10.				

APPENDIX

Code	SKILLS (Observable Behaviors, Not Traits/Values)
S1	
S2	
S3	
S4	
S5	
S6	
S7	
S8	

Code	Measurements	Code	Evaluation Methods	Education/Experience
M1		E1		1.
M2		E2		2.
M3		E3		3.
M4		E4		4.
M5		E5		5.
M6		E6		6.
M7		E7		7.
M8		E8		8.

APPENDIX

PERFORMANCE OBJECTIVES

EMPLOYEE:	POSITION:	DEPARTMENT:	SUPERVISOR:

TYPES OF PERFORMANCE OBJECTIVES:
PROJECT   PROCESS   BUSINESS-AS-USUAL   CORE VALUES

ORIGINATED:	REVISED:

OBJECTIVE	TYPE	TARGET DATE

EMPLOYEE SIGNATURE: DATE:

SUPERVISOR SIGNATURE: DATE:

Performance Action Plan

Employee:	Position:	Department:	Supervisor:

Performance Objective:	Originated:	Revised:

Actions/Milestones	Deliverables/Results	Required Resources
1.		
2.		
3.		
4.		

Risks, Impacts And Likelihood (High, Medium, Low)	Options And Recommendations
Risk: Impacts: Likelihood:	
Risk: Impacts: Likelihood:	
Risk: Impacts: Likelihood:	

APPENDIX

POSITION DESCRIPTION THOUGHT JOGGER

RESPONSIBILITIES

Here are some examples of position responsibilities that may apply at your organization *(note that all examples begin with an "action word")*.

- administer reports
- communicate inter- and intra-departmentally
- develop standards
- provide customer service
- develop employee skills
- manage projects
- plan budgets
- assure product quality
- research, analyze, design, develop
- supervise people
- plan strategically
- provide technical support
- produce graphics
- receive and distribute mail
- assemble products

APPENDIX

POSITION DESCRIPTION THOUGHT JOGGER

SKILLS

Use the action words from the following list to *"kick off"* a clear and succinct description of required skills in a *"Position Description."*

accept	condense	follow	model	research
accomplish	conduct	forecast	monitor	resolve
acknowledge	confront	formulate	motivate	respond
adhere	consolidate	gather	negotiate	restate
adjust	consult	guide	network	review
advise	control	help	offer	revise
agree	cooperate	hire	operate	reward
allocate	counsel	identify	order	schedule
analyze	create	implement	organize	select
anticipate	deal	incorporate	orient	sell
apply	decide	influence	participate	serve
assemble	define	inform	persuade	service
assess	delineate	initiate	place	share
assist	deliver	innovate	plan	solve
assure	design	inquire	prepare	speak
attend	describe	inspect	present	staff
audit	develop	inspire	price	stimulate
budget	direct	install	prioritize	summarize
building	discuss	instruct	process	support
chair	disseminate	interact	program	take
challenge	draft	interpret	project	talk
change	draw	interview	promote	teach
clarify	edit	inventory	propose	team-play
coach	encourage	invoice	provide	test
collaborate	ensure	keep	publish	time
collect	establish	lead	read	track
communicate	estimate	learn	reassure	train
compensate	evaluate	leverage	recognize	translate
compile	expedite	listen	recommend	understand
complete	experiment	maintain		update
comply	explain	manage	record	use
compose	extrapolate	mediate	report	validate
compromise	facilitate	meet	recruit	write
conceive	focus	mentor	repair	

APPENDIX

POSITION DESCRIPTION THOUGHT JOGGER

MEASUREMENTS

Agree upon specific ways you and your employee will measure and evaluate the employee's performance for each of his/her key responsibilities. *"Thought Joggers"* to help you develop specific performance measurements follow.

- Accuracy *(e.g., percentage of error-free work, reliability of data, confidence level, etc.)*
- Actual Effectiveness *(versus plan)*
- Autonomy *(i.e., independence)*
- Availability
- Clarity *(or conciseness)*
- Compliance
- Consistency
- Cost
- Currency *(e.g., how new is the information)*
- Customer Satisfaction *(or client relations)*
- Dimension *(e.g., verbal, written, on-line, etc.)*
- Ease Of Reference
- Employee Satisfaction
- Follow-Through
- Format
- Frequency
- Functionality
- Price
- Quality
- Quantity
- Responsiveness
- Scope
- Thoroughness *(or completeness)*
- Timeliness *(e.g., lead time, response time, down time, cycle time, etc.)*
- Yield *(e.g., profit, return on investment, etc.)*

APPENDIX

POSITION DESCRIPTION THOUGHT JOGGER

EVALUATION METHODS AND EDUCATION/EXPERIENCE

You can't always be there to observe each and every employee behavior. But, you can collect and share facts, figures, and other important information from written sources. You can also collect and share observations and perceptions from others through interviews, surveys, focus groups, etc. Examples follow.

Written Sources

- activity reports
- business plans
- calendars
- charts and graphs
- "critical incident" files
- customer letters
- employee development plans
- employee self-evaluations
- feedback planners
- Human Resources files and records
- operating manuals and references
- past performance appraisals
- performance objectives and action plans
- performance standards
- position descriptions
- policies and procedures
- project charts and schedules
- project status reports
- proposals and contracts
- strategic goals, objectives, and tactics
- surveys
- time sheets
- work group goals and objectives
- your personal notes

Human Resources

- associates
- clients
- consultants
- contractors
- coworkers
- internal/external customers (*including department users*)
- internal/external suppliers (*including other associates*)
- past/current managers
- peers
- senior managers
- subordinates (*direct reports*)
- witnesses to "*critical incidents*"

Education/Experience

- relevant and progressive job experience
- demonstrated experiences (*provide examples of accomplishments, project plans, analyses, presentation materials, flowcharts, diagrams, etc.*)
- academic course work or equivalent (*establish minimum qualifications by defining specific curriculum like "statistics" instead of "Business degree"*)
- relevant certifications, licenses, credentials, etc.
- relevant seminars, conferences, workshops, programs, etc.
- special projects, experiences, etc.

Professional And Personal Development Publications From Richard Chang Associates, Inc.

Designed to support continuous learning, these highly targeted, integrated collections from Richard Chang Associates, Inc. (RCA) help individuals and organizations acquire the knowledge and skills needed to succeed in today's ever-changing workplace. Titles are available through RCA, Jossey-Bass, Inc., fine bookstores, and distributors internationally.

Practical Guidebook Collection

Quality Improvement Series
Continuous Process Improvement
Continuous Improvement Tools, Volume 1
Continuous Improvement Tools, Volume 2
Step-By-Step Problem Solving
Meetings That Work!
Improving Through Benchmarking
Succeeding As A Self-Managed Team
Measuring Organizational Improvement Impact
Process Reengineering In Action
Satisfying Internal Customers First!

Management Skills Series
Interviewing And Selecting High Performers
On-The-Job Orientation And Training
Coaching Through Effective Feedback
Expanding Leadership Impact
Mastering Change Management
Re-Creating Teams During Transitions
Planning Successful Employee Performance
Coaching For Peak Employee Performance
Evaluating Employee Performance

High Performance Team Series
Success Through Teamwork
Building A Dynamic Team
Measuring Team Performance
Team Decision-Making Techniques

High-Impact Training Series
Creating High-Impact Training
Identifying Targeted Training Needs
Mapping A Winning Training Approach
Producing High-Impact Learning Tools
Applying Successful Training Techniques
Measuring The Impact Of Training
Make Your Training Results Last

Workplace Diversity Series
Capitalizing On Workplace Diversity
Successful Staffing In A Diverse Workplace
Team Building For Diverse Work Groups
Communicating In A Diverse Workplace
Tools For Valuing Diversity

Personal Growth And Development Collection

Managing Your Career in a Changing Workplace
Unlocking Your Career Potential
Marketing Yourself and Your Career
Making Career Transitions
Memory Tips For The Forgetful

101 Stupid Things Collection

101 Stupid Things Trainers Do To Sabotage Success
101 Stupid Things Supervisors Do To Sabotage Success
101 Stupid Things Employees Do To Sabotage Success
101 Stupid Things Salespeople Do To Sabotage Success
101 Stupid Things Business Travelers Do To Sabotage Success

About Richard Chang Associates, Inc.

Richard Chang Associates, Inc. (RCA) is a multi-disciplinary organizational performance improvement firm. Since 1987, RCA has provided private and public sector clients around the world with the experience, expertise, and resources needed to build capability in such critical areas as process improvement, management development, project management, team performance, performance measurement, and facilitator training. RCA's comprehensive package of services, products, and publications reflect the firm's commitment to practical, innovative approaches and to the achievement of significant, measurable results.

RCA Resources Optimize Organizational Performance

Consulting — Using a broad range of skills, knowledge, and tools, RCA consultants assist clients in developing and implementing a wide range of performance improvement initiatives.

Training — Practical, "real world" training programs are designed with a "take initiative" emphasis. Options include off-the-shelf programs, customized programs, and public and on-site seminars.

Curriculum And Materials Development — A cost-effective and flexible alternative to internal staffing, RCA can custom-develop and/or customize content to meet both organizational objectives and specific program needs.

Video Production — RCA's award-winning, custom video productions provide employees with information in a consistent manner that achieves lasting impact.

Publications — The comprehensive and practical collection of publications from RCA supports organizational training initiatives and self-directed learning.

Packaged Programs — Designed for first-time and experienced trainers alike, these programs offer comprehensive, integrated materials (including selected Practical Guidebooks) that provide a wide range of flexible training options. Choose from:

- Meetings That Work! ToolPAK™
- Step-By-Step Problem Solving ToolKIT™
- Continuous Process Improvement Packaged Training Program
- Continuous Improvement Tools, Volume 1 ToolPAK™
- Continuous Improvement Tools, Volume 2 ToolPAK™
- High Involvement Teamwork™ Packaged Training Program

RICHARD CHANG ASSOCIATES

World Class Resources. World Class Results.℠

Richard Chang Associates, Inc.
Corporate Headquarters
15265 Alton Parkway, Suite 300, Irvine, California 92618 USA
(800) 756-8096 • (949) 727-7477 • Fax: (949) 727-7007
E-Mail: info@rca4results.com • www.richardchangassociates.com

U.S. Offices in Irvine and Atlanta • Licensees and Distributors Worldwide